ADRIFT IN THE PACIFIC

The Fitzroy Edition of
JULES VERNE
Edited by I. O. Evans

★

A FLOATING CITY
THE BEGUM'S FORTUNE
FIVE WEEKS IN A BALLOON
DROPPED FROM THE CLOUDS
THE SECRET OF THE ISLAND
MICHAEL STROGOFF
THE DEMON OF CAWNPORE
TIGERS AND TRAITORS
FROM THE EARTH TO THE MOON
ROUND THE MOON
INTO THE NIGER BEND
THE CITY IN THE SAHARA
20,000 LEAGUES UNDER THE SEA
AT THE NORTH POLE
THE WILDERNESS OF ICE
THE MYSTERY OF ARTHUR GORDON PYM
 By Edgar Allan Poe and Jules Verne
JOURNEY TO THE CENTRE OF THE EARTH
PROPELLER ISLAND
FOR THE FLAG
BLACK DIAMONDS
THE MASTERLESS MAN
THE UNWILLING DICTATOR
THE CLAIM ON FORTY MILE CREEK
FLOOD AND FLAME
THE CLIPPER OF THE CLOUDS
MASTER OF THE WORLD
CARPATHIAN CASTLE
THE TRIBULATIONS OF A CHINESE GENTLEMAN
BURBANK THE NORTHERNER
TEXAR THE SOUTHERNER
LEADER OF THE RESISTANCE
INTO THE ABYSS

ADRIFT IN THE PACIFIC

by

JULES VERNE

Part I
of
TWO YEARS' HOLIDAY

Edited by
I. O. EVANS,
F.R.G.S.

LONDON
ARCO PUBLICATIONS
1964

First published 1964 by Arco Publications
© *Arco Publications 1964*

Printed in Northern Ireland by
W. & G. Baird, Ltd., Union Street, Belfast 1

CONTENTS

	INTRODUCTION	7
I	THE STORM	11
II	THE WRECK	23
III	CAST ADRIFT	35
IV	THE FIRST DAY ASHORE	43
V	THE VIEW FROM THE CAPE	53
VI	A SPELL OF RAIN	65
VII	THE EXPLORERS	77
VIII	THE CAVE	89
IX	FRANÇOIS BAUDOIN	99
X	THE RAFT	109
XI	A CAPTURE	123
XII	THE COLONY	133
XIII	WINTER QUARTERS	147
XIV	A JOURNEY NORTHWARDS	163
XV	BRAVO, BAXTER!	175

INTRODUCTION

ALTHOUGH JULES VERNE is commonly regarded —chiefly, I think, because many of his stories first appeared in Britain serialised in the *Boys' Own Paper*—as a 'juvenile' writer, he was in fact nothing of the kind. With one exception, the present work, his writings were intended not for young readers but for an adult public.

Indeed, he was not, strictly speaking, a fiction-writer at all; he did not aim merely to amuse and interest and 'thrill' his readers, and he had no ambition to form part of what is now called the 'entertainments industry'. He was first and foremost a *geographer* with general scientific interests, and almost all his work was didactic. He was anxious to impart to others the geographical and scientific information in which he revelled, and he chose a fictional form simply because this was the only way in which he could find a public.

The first of his 'extraordinary journeys', *Five Weeks in a Balloon*,* which at once raised him from obscurity to fame and fortune, was written because of his interest in the possibility of using balloons in geographical exploration, and he turned his original manuscript into a story at the express suggestion of his publisher. Its success encouraged him to use the same method for almost the whole of his life's work† and he was the virtual creator of two new

---
*Included in the present edition.
†The exceptions are a non-fictional history of exploration and discovery, and his share, another author having died, in an illustrated geography of France.

art-forms, science fiction itself and the story whose chief interest lies in its technical background.

This explains why many of his books are so grossly overloaded with technical detail which, in the expressive words of his biographer, Kenneth Allott, ' comforts and reassures the reader even as he skips the passage ', and which the judicious translator or editor is considerate enough to abridge or omit. It explains, too, the ' woodenness ' of certain of his characters, the superhuman wealth of information and their omnicompetence. It explains his almost shameless reliance on sheer coincidence, and his occasional scamping or omission of some episode almost vital to his story.

Yet, in spite of his obvious faults, Verne was a story-teller, and a story-teller of genius—otherwise his stories would never have lived. He had a sense of narrative, and he could write with a vividness that enabled him to hurry his heroes on from adventure to adventure and his readers from excitement to excitement. He had a sense of humour, and indeed of sardonic humour, with which to enliven his work. A few of his stories are marred by what seems national or racial prejudice, but these fortunately are exceptional, and his sympathies were in general very wide indeed. Above all, he had a deep religious faith which made his work sincere; he aimed not only to instruct his readers but to edify them.

In the present narrative Verne, writing expressly for young readers, took much trouble with the characterisation of his heroes. Numerous as these are, it will be seen that none of them is a mere ' passenger ' of whom nothing is known but the name; all are well enough characterised to be distinguishable by the dialogue, and all have their share in the adventures. Moreover, what Allott calls the 'schoolboy politics' which develop on Verne's 'earthly paradise', a desert island, are very cleverly handled.

The character of the French lad Briant is understood to be based on that of a schoolboy whom Verne knew—Aristide Briand, who later became Premier of France.

This book, although originally entitled *Two Years' Holiday* (*Deux Ans de Vacances*) first appeared in Britain as *Adrift in the Pacific*. Wildly inappropriate as this title is, however— for as will be seen it applies only to the first few chapters—it has been retained for the first part of the present edition simply to link this with its forerunner. The second part, which is entitled *Second Year Ashore*, describes the further adventures of these young Crusoes, who find they have to deal with troubles far more serious than the personal foibles of one or two of their own number.

I. O. E.

CHAPTER I

THE STORM

IT WAS March 9th, 1860, and eleven at night. The sea and sky were as one, and the eye could pierce only a few fathoms into the gloom. Through raging seas, whose waves broke with a livid light, a tiny ship was driving under almost bare poles.

She was a schooner of a hundred tons. Her name was the *Sleuth,* but it would have been sought in vain on her stern, for some accident had torn it away.

In this latitude, at the beginning of March, the nights are short. The day would dawn about five. But would the dangers that threatened the schooner grow less when the sun illumined the sky? Was not this vessel at the mercy of the waves? Undoubtedly; and only the calming of the billows and the lulling of the gale could save her from that most awful of shipwrecks—foundering in the open sea far from any coast where the survivors might find safety.

In her stern were three boys, one about fourteen, the two others about thirteen years of age; these, with a young negro some twelve years old, were at the wheel, and with their united strength they strove to check the lurches which threatened every instant to throw the vessel broadside on. It was a difficult task, for the wheel seemed as though it would turn in spite of all they could do, and hurl them against the bulwarks. Just before midnight such a wave came thundering against the stern that it was a wonder the rudder was not unshipped. The boys were thrown backwards by the shock, but they recovered themselves almost immediately.

'Has she still got steerage way, Briant?' one of them asked.

'Yes, Gordon,' answered Briant, who had coolly resumed his place. 'Hold on tight, Donagan,' he continued, ' and don't worry. There are others besides ourselves to look after. You aren't hurt, Moko?'

'No, Massa Briant,' answered the boy. 'But we must keep the yacht before the wind, or we'll be pooped.'

At this moment the door of the companion leading to the saloon was thrown open. Two little heads appeared above the level of the deck, and with them came the face of a dog, who gave a loud 'Whough! whough!'

'Briant! Briant!' shouted one of the youngsters. 'What's the matter?'

'Nothing, Iverson, nothing!' returned Briant. 'Get down again with Dole, and look sharp!'

'We're awfully frightened down here,' said the other boy, who was a little younger.

'All of you?' asked Donagan.

'Yes, all of us!' said Dole.

'Well, get back again,' Briant told them. 'Shut up; get under the bed-clothes; shut your eyes; and nothing will hurt you. There's no danger!'

'Look out,' exclaimed Moko. 'Here's another wave!'

A violent blow shook the vessel's stern. Fortunately the wave did not come on board, for if the water had swept down the companion, she would have been swamped.

'Get back, will you?' shouted Gordon. 'Go down, or I'll come after you!'

'Look here,' Briant told them, rather more gently. 'Go down, you young 'uns.'

THE STORM

The two heads disappeared, and at the same moment another boy appeared.

'Do you want us, Briant?'

'No, Baxter,' said Briant. 'You and Cross and Webb and Service and Wilcox stop with the kids; we four can manage.'

Baxter shut the door from within.

'Yes, all of us,' Dole had said.

But were there only boys on board this storm-driven schooner? Yes, only boys! And how many were there? Fifteen, counting Gordon, Briant, Donagan, and the negro. How did they come to be here? That you shall know shortly.

Was there no man on the yacht? Not a captain to command her? Not a sailor to give a hand in controlling her? Not a helmsman to steer in such a storm? No! Not one!

And more than that—there was nobody on board who knew her position! And on what ocean? The largest of all, the Pacific.

What, then, had happened? Had the schooner's crew disappeared in some catastrophe? Had the Malay pirates carried them off and left on board only this batch of boys? A yacht of a hundred tons ought to have a captain, a mate, and five or six men, and of these all that had been left was the negro boy! Where did the schooner hail from? How long had she been at sea? Whither was she bound? The boys might have been able to answer these questions had they been asked them by any captain hailing the schooner on her course; but there was neither steamer nor sailing-ship in sight, and, if there had been, she would have had quite enough to do to look after herself without assisting this yacht that the sea was throwing about like a raft.

Briant and his friends did their utmost to keep her straight ahead.

'What's to be done?' asked Donagan.

'All we can to save ourselves, Heaven helping us,' answered Briant, although now even the most energetic man might have despaired, for the storm was increasing in violence.

The gale was blowing in thunderclaps, as the sailors say, and the expression was only too accurate. The schooner had lost her mainmast, so that no trysail could be set under which she might have been more easily steered. The foremast still held, but the shrouds had stretched, and every minute it threatened to crash on to the deck. The fore-staysail had been split to ribbons, and kept up a constant cracking like rifle-fire. All that remained sound was the foresail, and this seemed as though it would go every moment, for the boys had not been strong enough to reef it. If it were to go, the schooner could not be kept before the wind, the waves would board her and she would go down.

Not an island had been sighted; and there could be no continent to the east. To run ashore would be terrible, but the boys did not fear its terrors so much as those of this interminable sea. A lee shore, with its shoals, its breakers, the terrible roaring waves beaten into surf by the rocks, would be at least firm ground, and not this raging ocean, which any minute might open under their feet. And so they looked ahead for some light to which they could steer.

But there was no light in that thick darkness!

Suddenly, about one o'clock, a fearful crash was heard above the roaring of the storm.

'There goes the foremast!' exclaimed Donagan.

'No,' Moko corrected him, 'it's the foresail blown clean away!'

'We must clear it,' said Briant. 'You stay at the wheel, Gordon, with Donagan; you, Moko, come and help me.'

Briant was not quite ignorant of things nautical. On his voyage out from Europe he had learnt a little seamanship, and that was why his companions, who knew none whatever, had left the schooner in his and Moko's hands.

Briant and the negro rushed forward. At all costs the foresail must be cut adrift, for it had caught and was bellying out in such a way that the schooner was in danger of capsizing. If that happened she could never be righted, unless the mast were cut away and the wire shrouds broken, and how could the boys manage that?

Briant and Moko set to work with remarkable judgment. Their object was to keep as much sail on the schooner as possible, so as to steer her before the wind as long as the storm lasted. They slacked off the halliards and let the sail down to within four or five feet of the deck: then they cut off the torn strips with their knives, secured the lower corners and made all snug. Twenty times, at least, they were in danger of being swept away by the waves.

Under her very small spread of canvas, the schooner could still be kept on her course, and though the wind had so little to take hold of, she was driven along at the speed of a torpedo-boat. The faster she went, the better. Her safety depended on her outspeeding the waves, so that none could follow and board her.

Briant and Moko were making their way back to the wheel when the companion door again opened and a boy's head again appeared. This time it was Jack, Briant's brother, and three years his junior.

'What do you want, Jack?' asked his brother.

'Come here! Come here!' said Jack. 'There's water in the saloon.'

Briant rushed down the companion-stairs. The saloon was confusedly lighted by a lamp, which the rolling swung backwards and forwards. Its light revealed a dozen boys on the couches. The youngest—there were some as young as eight—were huddling against each other in fear.

'There's no danger,' Briant assured them, wanting to give them confidence. 'We're all right. Don't be afraid.'

Then, holding a lighted lantern to the floor, he saw that some water was washing from side to side.

Where had this water come from? From a leak? That must be seen to at once.

Forward of the saloon was the day-saloon, then the dining-saloon, and then the crew's quarters.

Briant went through these in order, and found that the water came from the seas dashing over the bows and down the fore-companion, which had not been quite closed, and that it had been run aft by the pitching of the ship. There was no danger here.

He stopped to cheer up his companions as he went back through the saloon, and then returned to his place at the helm. The schooner was very strongly built, and had only just been re-coppered, so that she might withstand the waves for some time.

It was then about one. The darkness was deeper than ever, and the clouds still gathered; and more furiously than ever raged the storm. The yacht seemed to be rushing through a liquid mass that flowed above, beneath, and around her. The shrill cry of the petrel was heard. Did its appearance mean that land was near? No; for the petrel is often met with hundreds of miles at sea. And these storm-

THE STORM

birds found themselves powerless to struggle against the aerial current and were swept along like the schooner.

An hour later there was another report from the bow. What remained of the foresail had been split to ribbons, and the strips flew off into space like huge seagulls.

'No sail left!' exclaimed Donagan; 'and we can't possibly set another.'

'Well, it doesn't matter,' said Briant. 'We shan't get along so fast, that is all!'

'What an answer!' snapped Donagan. 'If that's your style of seamanship——'

'Look out for the wave astern!' said Moko. 'Lash yourselves, or you'll be swept overboard——'

The boy had not finished the sentence when several tons of water swept over the taffrail. Briant, Donagan, and Gordon were hurled against the companion, to which they managed to cling. But the negro had disappeared in the wave which swept the deck from stern to bow, carrying away the binnacle, the spare spars, and the three boats. The deck was cleared at one blow. But the water almost instantly flowed off, and the yacht was saved from sinking.

'Moko! Moko!' shouted Briant, as soon as he could speak.

'See if he's gone overboard,' said Donagan.

'No,' Gordon learnt out to leeward. 'No, I don't see him, and I don't hear him.'

'We must save him! Throw him a buoy! Throw him a rope!' said Briant.

And in a voice that rang clearly out in a few seconds' calm, he again shouted——'Moko! Moko!'

'Here! Help!' called the negro.

'He can't be in the sea,' said Gordon. 'His voice is coming from the bow.'

'I'll save him,' Briant declared.

And he crept forward along the heaving slippery deck, avoiding as best he might the blocks swinging from the loose ropes. The boy's voice was heard again, and then all was silent. By a great effort Briant reached the fore-companion.

He shouted. There was no response.

Had Moko been swept away into the sea since he gave his last cry? If so, he must be far astern now, for the waves could not carry him along as fast as the schooner was going. And then he was lost.

No! A feeble cry reached Briant, who hurried to the windlass in whose frame the foot of the bowsprit was fitted. There he found the negro wedged in the very angle of the bow. A halliard was gradually tightening round his neck. It had saved him when the wave was carrying him away. Was it to strangle him now?

Briant opened his knife, and, with some difficulty, managed to cut the rope. Moko was dragged aft, and as soon as he had strength enough to speak, 'Thanks, Massa Briant,' he said, and he at once took his place at the wheel, where the four did their utmost to keep the vessel safe from the enormous waves that pursued here, for these now ran faster than she did, and could easily have boarded her. But what could be done? It was impossible to set the least scrap of sail.

About four, the horizon would grow grey in the east, whither the schooner was being borne. With daybreak the storm might lull. Perhaps land might be in sight, and the boys' fate be settled in a few minutes!

About half-past four a diffused light began to appear overhead. Unfortunately the mist limited the view to less than a quarter of a mile. The clouds swept by with terrible speed. The storm had lost nothing of its fury; and only a short distance away the sea was hidden by the veil of spray from the raging waves. The schooner, at one moment mounting the wave-crest, at the next hurled into the trough, would have been shattered to pieces had she touched the ground.

The boys looked out at the chaos of wild water; they felt that if the calm were long in coming their situation would be desperate. The schooner could not possibly float for another day, for the waves would assuredly sweep away the companion and swamp her.

But suddenly there came a cry from Moko of 'Land! Land!'

Through a rift in the mist the boy thought he had seen the outline of a coast to the eastward. Was he mistaken? Nothing is more difficult than to recognise the vague lineaments of land, so easily confounded with those of the clouds.

'Land!' exclaimed Briant.

'Yes,' replied Moko. 'Land! To the eastward.' And he pointed towards a part of the horizon now hidden by vapour.

'Are you sure?' asked Donagan.

'Yes!—Yes!—Certain!' said Moko. 'If the mist opens again you look—there—a little to the right of the foremast —Look! Look!'

The mist began to open and rise from the sea. A few moments more, and the ocean reappeared for several miles ahead.

'Yes! Land! It's really land!' shouted Briant.

'And its very low,' added Gordon, who had just caught sight of the coast.

There was no room for doubt. A land—continent, or island—lay some five or six miles ahead. In that direction, from which the storm would not allow her to deviate, the schooner would be driven on it in less than an hour. That she would be smashed, particularly if the breakers stopped her before she reached the shore, there was every reason to fear. But the boys did not give that a thought. In this land, which had offered itself so unexpectedly to their sight, they saw, they could only see, a means of safety.

And now the wind was blowing with still greater strength; the schooner, carried along like a feather, was hurled towards the coast, which stood out like a line of ink on the whitish waste of sky. In the background was a cliff, about two hundred feet high; in the foreground was a yellowish beach ending towards the right in a rounded mass which seemed to belong to a forest further inland.

Ah! If the schooner could reach the sandy beach without hitting a line of reefs, if the mouth of a river would only offer her a refuge, her passengers might escape safe and sound!

Leaving Donagan, Gordon, and Moko at the helm, Briant went forward and scrutinised the land which he was nearing so rapidly. But in vain did he look for some place where the yacht could be run ashore without risk. There was the mouth of no river or stream, not even a sandbank, on which they could run her aground; but there was a line of breakers with the black heads of rock rising out of the surge, where the first shock would wrench the schooner to pieces.

Briant decided that it would be better for all his friends to be on deck when the crash came; opening the companion-door he shouted—

'Come on deck, every one of you!'

Immediately out jumped the dog, and then the eleven

boys one after the other; the sight of the mighty waves around them made the smallest of them yell with terror.

It was a little before six in the morning when the schooner reached the first line of breakers.

'Hold on, all of you!' shouted Briant, stripping off half his clothes, so as to be ready to help those whom the surf swept away when the vessel struck.

Suddenly there came a shock. The schooner had grounded under the stern. But the hull was not damaged, and no water rushed in. A second wave took her fifty feet further, just skimming the rocks that projected above the water-level in a thousand places. Then she heeled over to port and lay motionless, surrounded by the boiling surf.

She was not in the open sea, but a quarter of a mile from the beach.

CHAPTER II

THE WRECK

THE VEIL of mist had gone, and the eye could range over a wide expanse round the schooner. The clouds were still pursuing one another, and the storm had lost none of its strength. But it might be its last great effort—it was to be hoped so, for the state of affairs was as perilous now as it had been during the night, when the vessel was writhing in the open sea. Huddled together, the boys might well think themselves lost, as wave after wave came dashing against the nettings and covering them with spray. The shocks were so violent that the schooner could not possibly endure them long. But though at every blow she quivered throughout her frame, there did not seem to be a plank started from the time she grounded. Briant and Gordon had been below and reported that the water had not entered the hull; and they did their best to cheer up their comrades—particularly the little ones.

'Don't be afraid,' said Briant. 'The yacht is strongly built; the coast is near. Wait, and we'll try to reach the shore.'

'And why wait?' asked Donagan.

'Yes—why?' added another boy, about twelve years old, named Wilcox. 'Donagan is right. Why wait?'

'Because the sea is too high at present, and we'd be thrown out among the rocks,' answered Briant.

'And if the yacht goes to pieces?' asked a third boy, Webb, who was about as old as Wilcox.

'I don't think there's much fear of that,' Briant reassured him; ' at least till the tide turns. When it goes out we can see about saving ourselves'.

Briant was right. Although the tides are not very considerable in the Pacific, there is an appreciable difference of level between high and low water, so there would be an advantage in waiting a few hours, particularly if the wind dropped. The ebb might leave part of the reef dry, and it would then be less dangerous to leave the schooner and easier to cross the quarter of a mile to the beach.

Reasonable as was this advice, Donagan and two or three others were not prepared to follow it; they formed a small group in the bow and talked in whispers. During the schooner's voyage they had consented to obey Briant's orders, because of his knowledge of seamanship, but they had always meant to resume their freedom of action once they got ashore. And this was particularly the case with Donagan, who, in education and ability, considered himself a long way the superior of Briant and the rest. Briant happened to be of French birth, and, not unnaturally, the English were by no means disposed to knuckle under to him.

So Donagan, Wilcox, Webb and Cross stood in the bow and looked away across the sheet of foam, dotted with eddies, furrowed with currents which looked dangerous enough to satisfy any of them. The most skilful swimmer would have struggled in vain against the troubled tide that ebbed in the teeth of the boisterous wind. The advice to wait for an hour or two was only too sensible, and Donagan and his supporters had to yield to the evidence of their own eyes. They returned to the stern among the younger boys, just as Briant was saying to them—

'Above all things, don't let's separate! Let's all keep together, or we're lost.'

'Are you trying to lay down the law for us?' Donagan asked him.

'I'm not trying to do anything,' Briant replied, 'except what's necessary for the safety of us all.'

'Briant is quite right,' said Gordon, who never spoke without thinking, and generally took things in a cool quiet sort of way.

'Yes! Yes!' two or three of the youngsters joined in; they felt drawn towards Briant by instinct.

Donagan did not reply, but he and his friends kept away from the rest, and waited till it was time to begin saving themselves.

And now what was the land? Was it one of the isles of the Pacific Ocean or part of some continent? The question could not be answered, for the schooner was too near the shore for much of the coast-line to be seen. She was aground in a large bay, ended by two capes—that towards the north being high and hilly, that towards the south a long low spur. But beyond these capes did the sea trend off as if to surround an island?

If it happened to be an island, how were the boys to get away if they failed to float the schooner, which at high water might well be dashed to pieces on the reef? And if the island were a desert—and there are such in the Pacific—how could they support existence for any time on what provisions they might save from the wreck?

On a continent the chances of safety would be much greater, for it could be no other than South America. There, either in Chili or Bolivia, they would surely find assistance, if not immediately, at least within a few days of their getting to land. It is true that if the coast were that of the Pampas, some awkward adventures might have to be feared.

But now the main question was, how were they to get ashore? The weather was clear enough for all the details of the coast to be made out—the beach, the cliff behind, the clumps of trees at the base of the cliff—all were plain to see. Briant even saw the mouth of a small river some way to the right. The coast was not attractive, but verdure indicated a certain fertility; and beyond the cliff, and sheltered from the sea breezes, the soil might be better.

There was no sign that the land was inhabited: no house or hut, not even at the mouth of the river. The natives, if there were any, might perhaps prefer to live further from the shore, where they were exposed to such boisterous winds.

'I can't see any smoke,' said Briant, lowering the binoculars.

'And there isn't any boat on the beach,' Moko agreed.

'How could there be, if there isn't a harbour?' asked Donagan.

'There doesn't have to be a harbour,' Gordon explained. 'Fishing-boats could lay up the river mouth, and the storm may have made the people take them up the river.'

Gordon was quite right: there was no sign of a boat to be seen, and the whole coast seemed uninhabited.

The tide was going out—very slowly, it is true—for the wind was driving it back. But the wind was falling and edging more to the north-west, and everything ought to be in readiness when the reef offered a practicable passage.

It was nearly seven. Everyone was busy bringing up on deck such things as were of first importance, leaving the others to be collected when the sea washed them ashore. There was on board a large store of preserved provisions, some of which were made up into packages for the older boys to take with them.

But for this to be done the reef ought to be dry. Would the tide be low enough to leave the beach dry up to the rocks? Briant and Gordon watched the sea anxiously. With the change in the wind it had become calmer, and the boiling of the surf began to subside; and it was now easy to note the lower level of the water round the rocks. The schooner showed the effects of this by giving a stronger list to port. It was feared, if the heeling continued, that she would go right over on her side, for like all modern high speed yachts she was narrow and deep. If she did, if the water reached the deck before the boys could leave her, matters would be serious.

What a pity the boats had been carried away in the storm! They were large enough to hold everyone on board, and Briant and his comrades could have tried to reach the shore in them, and afterwards to take many things from the wreck, much that would now have to be left. If the schooner broke up during the night, would the wreckage be any use after it had been knocked about among the rocks? What would become of the food? Would the boys have to trust to whatever the island might produce? It was certainly a pity that they had lost the boats.

Suddenly there was a shout from the bow. Baxter had made an important discovery. The yawl, instead of having been washed away, was foul of the bowsprit and undamaged. It could hold only five or six, it is true, but it would be very useful indeed if the tide did not ebb far enough to leave a dry passage to land.

But here again a discussion broke out, with Briant and Donagan on opposite sides. As soon as the yawl was found, Donagan, Wilcox, Webb, and Cross had taken possession of her.

'What are you doing?' Briant demanded.

'What we choose,' Wilcox told him.

'Are you going off in that boat?'

'Yes,' said Donagan, 'and it will take more than you to stop us.'

'I shall stop you,' Briant declared; 'I and the ones you're going to leave behind.'

'Leave behind!' said Donagan contemptuously. 'So that's what you think, is it? I'm not going to leave anybody behind, you see! We're going to the beach and then one of us will bring the yawl back——'

'And if you can't get back?' said Briant, with difficulty keeping his temper. 'If she gets stove in on the rocks?—'

'Come on!' said Webb, pushing Briant aside, 'Let's get her off!'

Briant caught hold of the boat as they were trying to launch her.

'You shan't go,' he declared again.

'We'll see about that,' Donagan replied.

'You shan't go,' said Briant. 'This boat is for the youngsters, if the tide isn't low enough to let them walk ashore.'

'Leave it alone,' said Donagan angrily. 'I tell you, Briant, you shan't stop us.'

'And I tell you, Donagan, that I shall.'

So there was to be a fight over it: Wilcox, Webb, and Cross took Donagan's part; and Baxter, Service and Garnett were backing up Briant, when Gordon intervened. He was the oldest and coolest of the lot, and he showed his good sense by intervening in favour of Briant:

'Come, come, Donagan, don't be in such a hurry! Can't

THE WRECK

you see the water's very rough and that there's a chance of your losing the boat?'

'I won't stand Briant domineering over us as he's been doing lately,' protested Donagan.

'Hear! Hear!' Cross and Webb chimed in.

'I'm not domineering over anybody,' Briant protested; 'but I won't let anybody act for himself at the expense of everybody else.'

'We think just as much of others as you do,' said Donagan; 'and when we're ashore—'

'Which we aren't just yet! said Gordon. 'Come, Donagan, don't be so obstinate; leave the boat alone till there's a better chance!'

The efforts of the peacemaker were successful—as they had been more than once before—and for a time the boys left the boat alone.

The tide had now gone down a couple of feet. Was there a channel through the breakers? Briant went forward to see. Mounting the starboard shrouds, he sat on the crosstrees. Through the reef a channel could be traced by the rock points sticking up out of the water on each side. But there were too many eddies along it to think of venturing along it in the boat at present. Better wait a little until the outgoing tide left it practicable.

From the cross-trees Briant carefully studied the coast in front of him. There were no signs of inhabitants in the bay, which was about eight miles long.

After being aloft half an hour, he returned to report what he had seen. Donagan and his supporters listened without saying anything. Not so Gordon, who asked: 'It was about six wasn't it, when the yacht grounded?'

'Yes,' said Briant.

'And how long is the tide running out?'

'Five hours, I think. Isn't it, Moko?' replied Briant.

'Yes, five or six hours,' said Moko.

'That would make it eleven,' Gordon meditated aloud 'for the best time for us to try.'

'That's what I thought' agreed Briant.

'Well, let's have it all ready by then,' Gordon decided. 'And now let's have something to eat. If we have to take to the water, let it be after we've had a meal.'

The suggestion was received with much applause, and acted upon immediately. With the biscuits and the jam the youngsters forgot their troubles, and as they had had nothing to eat for twenty-four hours, they ate away steadily as if they never meant to stop.

After a time Briant went forward and took another long look at the rocks.

How slowly the tide seemed to go out! And yet the depth of water must be decreasing, for the yacht was heeling over more and more. Moko got out the lead-line and found he touched bottom at eight feet. Would the schooner be left high and dry? He did not think so, and he took an opportunity of telling Briant on the quiet, so as to alarm nobody.

Briant went and consulted with Gordon. Evidently the northerly wind prevented the tide running out as far as usual in calm weather.

'What's to be done?' said Gordon.

'I don't know,' replied Briant. 'What a nuisance it is that we're only boys when we ought to be men!'

'It is rather!' Gordon agreed. 'But necessity, you know, may bring us up to the mark. Never despair! We'll be all right. We must do something.'

'Yes; we must do something. If we don't get away from the ship before the tide comes back, we'll be done for.'

THE WRECK

'That's true enough, for she'll go to pieces. We must leave her somehow.'

'Yes, somehow!'

'Couldn't we make a raft?'

'I thought of that, but nearly all the spars went overboard in the storm. We can't break up the deck to make a raft with the planks, for we won't have time. There's only the boat, and the sea's too rough for her. All I can see is to get a rope across the reef, and fasten it to one of those rocks over there. We might get them all ashore that way.'

'Who'll take the rope?'

'I will,' Briant replied.

'And I'll help you!' Gordon replied.

'No. I'll go alone.'

'Won't you take the boat?'

'That would risk losing her. Better keep her as a last resource.'

But before starting on this dangerous plan Briant took another precaution. There were a few life-belts, and these he made the smaller boys put on. If they had to leave the wreck while the water was too deep for them to wade, the belts would keep them afloat, and the bigger boys, as they clung to the rope, could push them ashore.

It was then a quarter-past ten. In forty-five minutes it would be low water. At the schooner's bow there was not more than four or five feet of water; but it seemed as though only a few inches more would run out. Sixty yards away the water shallowed considerably, as could be seen by its colour and by the numerous rocks sticking up out of it.

To cross this sixty yards was the difficulty. If Briant could get a rope firmly fixed to one of the pointed rocks, and stretch it taut with the help of the windlass, all would get off in safety. And along the rope they could slide the packages and provisions and other articles from the wreck. But it was a risky undertaking, and Briant would allow no one to attempt it but himself.

He chose a rope of moderate size, and, slipping off his clothes, tied it round his waist.

'Now, come along there,' Gordon shouted. 'Stand by to pay out the rope.'

Donagan and his friends came forward with the rest, and stood ready to slack the rope out gently from the coil so as to ease off the weight as much as possible.

As Briant was about to plunge into the sea his brother ran up screaming: 'Brother! Brother!'

'Don't worry, Jack, don't worry about me!' was the reply, and in another moment Briant was on the surface of the sea, swimming strongly with the rope behind him.

In a calm the task would not have been easy, for the surf beat furiously among the rocks. Currents and counter-currents prevented the brave boy from keeping a straight line, and when he entered them he could only with difficulty make his way through. Gradually he made his way towards the beach, but it was evident that his strength was failing. He had not gone twenty yards from the schooner when he entered a whirlpool caused by the meeting of two streams of surf. If he could get round it or through it, all might be well, for the sea beyond was calm. He tried to pass it on the left hand, but the attempt was a failure: a strong swimmer in the prime of life would have tried in vain. The whirlpool seized him, and drew him irresistibly to the centre.

'Help! Pull! Pull!' he shouted, and then he disappeared.

On the schooner terror was at its height.

'Haul away!' said Gordon coolly.

And the boys hauled as if for their lives, and in less than a minute Briant was on board—unconscious, it is true, but soon restored to life and back in his brother's arms.

That attempt had failed. What was to be done now? Were they to wait? To wait for what? Help? And where was help to come from? It was now past noon, and the tide began to make, the surf increasing as the water rose. And as it was new moon the tide would be higher than the evening before. And the wind had gone down but little; the schooner might be lifted from its rocky bed, strike again, and be shattered on the reef! Then none of them would survive! And yet nothing could be done!

In the stern the young boys gathered round the older ones, and watched the waters rise, and the rocks disappear beneath the surf. The wind had gone round to the west again, and beat full on the shore. As the water deepened the waves rose, and rolled and broke up against her. By two o'clock the schooner had recovered from her heel and was upright; her bow was free and being dashed up and down on the rocks, while her stern remained firmly fixed. Soon she began to roll from side to side and the boys had to cling together to keep from being thrown overboard.

Suddenly a foaming mountain came rolling in from the open sea, and rose a few feet from the vessel's stern. It was over twenty feet high; it rushed along with the fury of a torrent; it covered the reef; it lifted the schooner from the rocks, swept her onward, and without even grazing them: in less than a minute, amid the roaring mass of water, the wreck was carried to the beach, and laid on the sand within a couple of hundred feet of the trees at the foot of the cliff. And there it remained, while the sea flowed back and left it high and dry.

CHAPTER III

CAST ADRIFT

CHARMAN'S BOARDING-SCHOOL was then one of the largest in Auckland, New Zealand. It boasted about a hundred pupils belonging to the best families in the colony, and the course of study and the management were the same as in high-class schools at home.

On February 15th, 1860, in the afternoon, a crowd of boys and their relatives came out of the schoolhouse, merry and happy as birds just escaped from their cage. It was the beginning of the holidays. Two months of independence; two months at liberty! And for some of the boys there was the prospect of a sea voyage which they had talked about for months. How the others envied those who were to go on this cruise which was to circumnavigate New Zealand! The schooner had been chartered by the boys' friends, and fitted out for a voyage of six weeks. She belonged to the father of one of the boys, William H. Garnett, an old merchant captain in whom everyone felt confidence. A subscription raised among the parents would cover the expenses; and great was the joy of the young folks, who would have found it difficult to spend their holidays better.

The fortunate boys were of all ages from eight to fourteen. With the exception of the Briants, who were French, and Gordon, who was an American, they were all English.

Donagan and Cross were the sons of rich landholders, who occupy the highest social rank in New Zealand. They were cousins; both were a little over thirteen and both in the fifth form. Donagan was something of a dandy and undoubtedly the foremost pupil in the school. He was clever and hardworking, and his fondness for study and desire to excel easily maintained his position. A certain aristocratic arrogance had gained him the nickname of Lord Donagan, and his imperious character made him strive to take command wherever he might find himself. Hence this rivalry between him and Briant, and it had become keener than ever since circumstances had increased Briant's influence over his companions. Cross was quite an ordinary sort of boy, distinguished by his constant admiration for everything his cousin said or did.

Baxter, too, was a fifth-form boy. Thirteen years of age, a cool, thoughtful, ingenious fellow, who could do almost anything with his hands, he was the son of a merchant who was not particularly well off.

Webb and Wilcox, both about twelve and a half, were in the fourth form. They were not particularly bright, and were rather inclined to be quarrelsome. Their fathers were wealthy men, and held high rank among the magistracy of New Zealand.

Garnett and Service were in the third form. They were both twelve years old. One was the son of a retired merchant captain, the other's father was well-to-do. The families were very intimate, and Service and Garnett were almost inseparable. They were good-hearted boys, not overfond of work, and if they had been given the key of the fields, as the French call it, they would not have let it rest idle in their pockets. Garnett had an over-mastering passion—he loved an accordion! And he took it with him on board the yacht, to occupy his spare time in a way befitting a sailor's son. Service was the school wag, the liveliest and noisiest of the lot, a devourer of travellers' tales, and a worshipper of *Robinson Crusoe* and the *Swiss Family Robinson*, which he knew by heart.

Among the boys, two were nine years old. The first of these was Jenkins, the son of the secretary of the New Zealand Royal Society; the other was Iverson, whose father was the minister of St. Paul's Church. Jenkins was in the third form, Iverson in the second; but both were good boys. Dole and Costar were each a year younger than Iverson, and were the sons of military officers. They were both little fellows, Dole very obstinate, and Costar very greedy. Both were in the first form, and both knew how to read and write.

Of the three others, Gordon, the American, was about fourteen, and his somewhat angular build already betrayed his Yankee origin. Slightly awkward, and a little heavy, he was far and away the steadiest boy in the fifth form; though there was nothing very brilliant about him, he had a clear head and a strong fund of common sense. His tastes were serious, and he was of an observant character and cool temperament. He was methodical even to the slightest detail, classifying his ideas in his head like the things in his desk, where everything was classified, docketed, and entered in its special notebook. His companions liked him, and recognised his good qualities. He was a native of Boston, but, having neither father nor mother, he had been taken care of by his guardian, a consular agent who had made his fortune and settled in New Zealand.

Briant and his brother were the sons of a French engineer, who, for two years and a half, had been employed in charge of the works for draining a marsh in the centre of the North Island. Briant was thirteen, an intelligent lad with no particular liking for hard work, and figuring with undesirable frequency at the wrong end of the fifth form.

When he wanted to, however, he speedily rose in the class, thanks to his facility of assimilation and his remarkable memory. He was bold, enterprising, active, quick at repartee, and good-natured. He was generally liked, and when the schooner was in difficulties his companions, with a few exceptions, did as he told them, principally from his having gained some nautical knowledge on his way out from Europe. Though young, he was ' a true Frenchman.'

His young brother, Jack, would have been the school jester had it not been for Service. He spent his time chiefly in inventing new modes of mischief for his schoolfellows' benefit, and being consequently in hot water; but for some reason his conduct on the vessel differed from what it had been at school.

Such were the schoolboys whom the storm had cast ashore in the Pacific. During the cruise round New Zealand the schooner was to have been commanded by Garnett's father, one of the best yachtsmen in Australasia. Many times had the schooner been sighted off the coast of Australia from the southernmost cape of Tasmania to Torres Straits, and even in the seas of the Moluccas and the Philippines, which are so dangerous to vessels even of greater tonnage. But she was a well-built boat, handy, staunch, and fit to keep the sea in all weathers.

The crew was to have consisted of the mate, six sailors, a cook and a boy, Moko, the young negro of twelve, whose family had been in the service of a well-known New Zealander for many years. And we ought to mention Fan, a dog of American extraction, which belonged to Gordon, and which never left her master.

The day of departure had been fixed for 15th February. The schooner lay moored at the end of Commercial Pier. The crew was not on board when, on the evening of the

14th, the young passengers embarked. Captain Garnett was not expected till the last moment, and the mate and the boy received Gordon and his companions, the men having gone ashore to take a parting glass. When the yacht had been cleared of visitors, and the boys had all gone to bed, so as to be ready early next morning for the start, the mate decided that he would go up into the town and look for his men, leaving Moko in charge. And Moko was too tired to keep awake . . .

What had happened after the mate left was a mystery, but, accidentally or purposely, the moorings had got cast off without anyone on board being the wiser.

It was a dark night. The land-breeze was strong, and the tide running out, and away went the schooner out to sea.

When Moko awoke he found they were adrift!

His shouts brought up Gordon, Briant, Donagan and a few of the others from below, but there was nothing they could do. They called for help in vain. None of the harbour lights were visible. The yacht was right out in the gulf three miles from land.

At the suggestion of Briant and Moko, the boys tried to get sail on the vessel so as to beat back into harbour. But the sail was too heavy for them to set properly, and the result was that the schooner, instead of keeping her head up, dropped dead away to leeward. Cape Colville was doubled, and the strait between Great Barrier Island and the mainland run through, and soon the schooner was off to the eastward, many miles from New Zealand.

This was serious. There could be no help from the land. If a vessel were to come in search, several hours must elapse before she could catch them, even supposing that she could find them in the darkness. And even when day came, how could she descry so small a craft on the high sea? If the wind did not change, all hope of returning to land must be given up. There remained only the chance of being spoken by some vessel on her way to a New Zealand port. And to meet this, Moko hastened to hoist a lantern at the foremast head. And then all that could be done was to wait for daylight.

Many of the smaller boys were still asleep, and it was thought best not to wake them.

Several attempts were made to bring the schooner up in the wind, but all were useless. Her head fell off immediately, and away she went drifting to the eastward.

Suddenly a light was sighted two or three miles off. It was a white masthead light, showing a steamer under way. Soon the side lights, red and green, rose above the water, and the fact of their being seen together showed that the steamer was steering straight for the yacht .

The boys shouted in vain. The wash of the waves, the roar of the steam blowing off, and the moan of the rising wind united to drown their voices. But if they could not hear the cries, the look-outs might see the light at the schooner's foremast? It was a last chance, and unfortunately, in one of her jerky pitches, the halliard broke and the lantern fell into the sea, and there was nothing to show the presence of the schooner, which the steamer was steering straight down upon at the rate of twelve knots.

In a few seconds she had struck the other vessel, and would have sunk her, had she not taken her on the slant close to the stern; as it was she carried away only part of the name-board.

The shock had been so feeble that the steamer kept on, leaving the schooner to the mercy of the approaching storm. It is occasionally true, unfortunately, that captains do not trouble about stopping to help a vessel they have run into. But in this case some excuse could be made, for those on board the steamer felt nothing of the collision, and saw nothing of the schooner in the darkness.

Drifting before the wind, the boys might well think they were lost. When day came the wide horizon was deserted. In the Pacific, ships bound from Australia to America, or from America to Australia, take a more notherly or more southerly route than their own. Not one was sighted, and although the wind moderated occasionally, yet it never ceased blowing from the westward.

How long this drifting was to last, neither Briant nor his comrades knew. In vain they tried to get the schooner back into New Zealand waters. It was under these conditions that Briant, displaying an energy superior to his age, began to exercise an influence over his companions, to which even Donagan submitted. Although with Moko's help he could not succeed in getting the schooner to the westward, he could, and did, manage to keep her navigable. He did not spare himself. He watched night and day. He swept the horizon for any chance of safety. And he threw overboard several bottles containing an account of what had happened to the schooner; it was a slender chance, doubtless, but he did not care to neglect it.

A few hours after the vessel had left Hauraki Gulf, the storm arose, and for two weeks it raged with unusual impetuosity. Assaulted by enormous waves, and escaping a hundred times from being overwhelmed by the mountains of water, the schooner had now gone ashore on some unknown land in the Pacific.

What was to be the fate of these shipwrecked schoolboys? Where was help to come from if they could not help themselves?

Their families had only too good reason to suppose that

they had been swallowed up by the sea. When it was found that the vessel had disappeared the alarm was given, and there is no need to dwell on the consternation the news produced.

Without losing an instant, the harbour-master sent out two small steamers in search, with orders to explore the gulf and some miles beyond it. All that night, though the sea grew rough, the little steamers sought in vain; and when day came and they returned to Auckland, it was to deprive the unfortunate relatives of every hope. They had not found the schooner, but they had found the planking knocked away in collision by the *Quito*—a collision of which those on board the *Quito* knew nothing.

And on the planking were three or four letters of the schooner's name.

It seemed certain that the vessel had met with disaster, and gone down with all on board a dozen miles off New Zealand.

CHAPTER IV

THE FIRST DAY ASHORE

THE SHORE was deserted, as Briant had discovered when he was on the foremast cross-trees. For an hour the schooner lay on her bed of sand. No native could be seen, nor was there any sign of house or hut either under the trees in front of the cliff or on the banks of the rivulet, now filled with the waters of the rising tide. There was not even the print of a human foot on the beach, which the tide had bordered with a long line of seaweed. At the mouth of the river no fishing-boat was to be seen, and no smoke arose in the air along the whole curve of the bay between the northern and southern capes.

The first idea that occurred to Briant and Gordon was to get through the trees and climb the cliffs behind.

'We're on land, that's something!' said Gordon; 'but what's this land which seems so uninhabited?'

'The important thing is that it isn't uninhabitable,' answered Briant. 'We've got enough food and ammunition for some time. We want a shelter of some sort, and we must find one—at least for the kids.'

'Yes. Right you are!'

'As to finding out where we are,' Briant continued, 'there'll be time enough for that when we have nothing else to do. If it's a continent, we may perhaps be rescued. If it's an island! an uninhabited island—well, we shall see! Come, Gordon, let's be off on our exporation.'

They soon reached the edge of the trees, which ran off

on the slant from the cliff to the right bank of the stream, three or four hundred yards above its mouth.

In the wood there was no sign of man, not a track, not a footpath. Old tree-trunks, fallen through age, lay on the ground, and the boys sank to their knees in the carpet of dead leaves. But the birds flew away in alarm as if they had learnt that men was their enemy, so it was likely that if the island were not inhabited, it was occasionally visited by the natives of some neighbouring territory.

In ten minutes the boys were through the wood, which grew thicker where the rocks at the back rose like a wall for nearly a hundred feet. Was there any break or hollow in this wall in which they could find a refuge? A cave sheltered from the gales by the curtain of trees, and beyond the reach of the sea even during the storms, would be the very place for the boys to take up their quarters until a careful exploration enabled them to move further inland.

Unluckily the cliff was as free from irregularity as the wall of a fortification. There was no cave, nor was there any place where the cliff could be climbed. To reach the interior the shore would have to be followed until the cliff ended.

For half an hour Briant and his companions kept on to southward along the foot of the cliff, then they reached the right bank of the stream, which came meandering in from the east. They were standing on the right bank, under the shade of the lofty trees; but the left bank bordered a country of very different aspect; flat and verdureless, it looked like a wide marsh extending to the southern horizon. Disappointed in their hope of reaching the top of the cliff whence they might have had a view of many miles over the country, the boys returned to the wreck.

Donagan and a few others were strolling among the rocks, while Jenkins, Iverson, Dole and Costar were amusing themselves collecting shellfish. The explorers reported the result of their journey. Until a more distant expedition could be undertaken, it seemed best not to abandon the wreck, which, although stove in below and heeling considerably, would do very well as a temporary dwelling-place. The deck had been half torn up forward, but the saloons gave ample shelter against a storm. To the very great satisfaction of the smaller boys, the galley had not been damaged at all.

It was lucky for them that they had no need to carry the salvage from the wreck to the shore. If the schooner had remained on the reef, it is difficult to see how the many useful articles could have been saved. The sea would soon have broken up the wreck, and provisions, weapons, clothes, bedding, and cooking gear would have been scattered in confusion on the beach. Fortunately the schooner had been swept on to the sand, in such a state, it is true, that she would never float again, but still habitable, at least for a time. Before she became useless as a dwelling the boys might hope to find some town or village, or, if the island were deserted, some cave in the rocks where they might make their home.

That very day they set to work to make the schooner comfortable. A rope-ladder on the starboard side gave easy access to the beach. Moko, who as a cabin-boy knew something of cooking, took charge of the galley, and, helped by Service, proceeded to prepare a meal which, thanks to good appetites, gave general satisfaction; even Jenkins, Iverson, Dole and Costar became quite lively. Jack alone was miserable; his character seemed to have completely altered, but to all his companions' inquiries he gave evasive replies.

Thoroughly tired out after so many days and nights of danger, the need of a good sound sleep was obvious to all. The youngsters were the first to find their way to the saloon, and the others soon followed. Briant, Gordon and Donagan took it in turns to keep watch. Might not some wild beasts put in an appearance? Or even a band of natives, who would be more formidable? But neither came. The night passed without an alarm of any kind; and when the sun rose the boys joined in a prayer of thanks to God for their deliverance from peril, and started work.

The first thing was to make a list of the provisions, and then of the weapons, instruments, utensils, clothes, tools, and so forth. The food question was serious, for it seemed they were on a desert island. They would have to trust to fishing and shooting, if there were anything to shoot. Donagan, who was a capital shot, had seen nothing yet but the birds on the reef and beach. But to be reduced to feeding on sea-birds was not a pleasant prospect, and they needed to know how long the schooner's provisions would last if managed with care.

Except for the biscuits, of which there was a large store, the preserves, hams, meat biscuits—made of flour, minced pork, and spice— corned beef, salt beef, and sea stores generally, could not last longer than two months. So from the very first they must have recourse to the products of the country, and keep the provisions in case they had to journey some hundreds of miles to reach a port on the coast or a town in the interior.

'Suppose some of these things have been damaged?' asked Baxter. 'If the sea-water got into the hold—'

'We'll see about that when we open the cases that look

as if they've been knocked about,' said Gordon. 'If we were to cook them up again, they might do.'

'I'll look after that,' said Moko.

'The sooner the better,' Briant told him 'for the first day or two we'll have to live entirely on these things.'

'And why shouldn't we start today?' asked Wilcox, 'and see if we can't find some eggs among those rocks to the northward?'

'Yes! That's it!' Dole agreed.

'And why shouldn't we go fishing?' asked Webb. 'Aren't there any fishing-lines on board? Who'll go fishing?'

'I will! I will!' the youngsters chorused.

'All right,' said Briant. 'But no playing about; we only give the lines to the ones who mean business.'

'Don't get excited,' said Iverson. 'We'll be as steady as—'

'But look here,' put in Gordon; 'first we must make a list of what there is on board. We have other things to think of besides what there is to eat.'

'We can go and get a few oysters for lunch,' said Service.

'Ah! That'll do,' Gordon agreed. 'Off you go in twos and threes; and, Moko, you go with them.'

The negro could be trusted. He was willing, clever and plucky, and would probably be of great use. He was attached to Briant, who did not conceal his liking for him.

'Come on!' said Jenkins.

'Aren't you going with them, Jack?' asked Briant.

Jack replied in the negative.

Jenkins, Dole, Costar, and Iverson then went off with Moko in charge, and scrambled up on to the reef which the sea had just left dry. In the cracks and crannies they might come across many molluscs, mussels, clams or even oysters, which, either raw or cooked, would form a welcome reinforcement. Away they went, running and jumping, and evidently looking on the expedition as one of pleasure rather than of work; at their age they remembered little of the trials they had passed through, and thought less of the dangers to come.

As soon as they had gone the elder boys began to search the wreck; Donagan, Cross, Wilcox, and Webb devoted themselves to the weapons, ammunition, clothes, bedding, tools, and utensils, while Briant, Garnett, Baxter, and Service took stock of the drinkables. As each article was called out Gordon entered it in his note-book.

It was found that the schooner had a complete set of spare sails and rigging of all sorts, cordage, cables, hawsers and so forth, and if she could have been got afloat again she could have been completely refitted. These best quality sails and new cordage would never again be used on the sea; but they would come in useful in other ways. A few fishing appliances, hand-lines, and deep-sea lines, figured in the inventory, and very valuable they would be, for fish were abundant.

The list of weapons in the note-book included eight central-fire fowling-pieces, a long-range duck-gun, and twelve revolvers, with 300 cartridges for the breech-loaders, two barrels of gunpowder, each of twenty-five pounds, and a large quantity of lead, small shot and bullets. The storeroom also contained a few rockets for night signalling, and thirty cartridges and projectiles for the two small cannon, which they hoped would not have to be used in repulsing a native attack.

The cooking utensils and such like were enough, even if the stay were to be lengthy. Though a good deal of the

THE FIRST DAY ASHORE

crockery had been smashed when the yacht ran ashore on the reef, yet enough remained, and these amenities were not absolutely necessary. There were more valuable things, such as garments of flannel, cloth, cotton and linen, enough to give a change for each variation in the climate. And if the land were in the same latitude as Auckland, which was likely, as the vessel had run before a westerly wind all the time, the boys might expect a hot summer and a very cold winter. In the seamen's chests were trousers, cloth jackets, water-proofed coats, and thick jerseys, that could be made to fit big or little, and enable them to defy the rigours of the winter. If they had to abandon the schooner, each could take away with them a complete set of bedding, for the bunks were well supplied with mattresses, sheets, blankets, pillows, and quilts, and with care these would last a long time.

A long time! That might mean for ever. In Gordon's note-book there was also a list of the instruments; two aneroid barometers, a spirit thermometer, two chronometers, several copper speaking-trumpets, three telescopes of short and long range, a binnacle compass and two smaller ones, a storm-glass indicating the approach of tempestuous weather, several British ensigns and jacks, and a set of signalling flags. And there was also a Halkett boat—a little india-rubber canoe which folds up like a bag, and is large enough to take one person across a river or lake.

There were plenty of tools in the carpenter's chest, bags of nails, screws, and iron nuts and clamps of all sorts for repairing the vessel. Thread and needles were not wanting, for the mothers had prepared for frequent mendings. There was no risk of being deprived of fire, for without reckoning matches there were enough tinder-boxes and tinder to last for a long time.

There were some large-scale charts, but only for the coast of New Zealand, and useless for the region where they had been wrecked; but luckily Gordon had brought a general atlas, and the yacht's library included several good works of travel and manuals of science, to say nothing of *Robinson Crusoe* and the *Swiss Family Robinson* which Service had saved from the wreck as Camoens saved his *Lusiad*. And of course Garnett had taken good care that his famous accordion had come off safe and sound. There were pens and pencils, and ink and paper, and an almanack for 1860, which was at once handed over to Baxter for him to cancel each day as it elapsed.

'It was on the tenth of March,' he said, 'that we came ashore. Well, out goes the tenth of March and all the days before it.'

In the strong-box of the yacht there was about £500 in gold, which might come in useful if the boys reached some port from which they could get home.

Gordon took careful stock of the casks stowed in the hold, of which many, containing spirits, ale, or wine, had been stove in while the schooner was being dashed about on the reef. But there were still a hundred gallons of claret and sherry, fifty gallons of gin, brandy, and whisky, and forty hogsheads of ale, besides thirty unbroken bottles of liqueurs in straw coverings.

So that, for some time at least, the fifteen survivors of the schooner were in no fear of starvation. It remained to be seen if the country would yield anything to economise their provisions. If it were an island on which the storm had thrown them, they could hardly hope to get away unless a ship were to appear and see their signals. To repair the vessel and make good the damage to the hull would be a task beyond their power, and require tools they did not possess. To build a new boat out of the ruins of the old one did not enter their minds; as they knew nothing of navigation, how could they cross the Pacific to get back to New Zealand? In the schooner's boats they might perhaps have got away; but the boats had gone, except the yawl, and that was fit only for sailing along the coast at best.

About noon, the youngsters returned, headed by Moko. They had at last quietened down and set seriously to work, and they had brought back a good store of shellfish, which the cabin-boy undertook to prepare. As to eggs, there ought to be a great quantity, for Moko had noticed innumerable rock pigeons of an edible kind nesting on the higher ledges of the cliff.

'That's all right,' said Briant. 'One of these mornings we'll go out after them, and get a lot.'

'We're sure to do that,' agreed Moko. 'Three or four shots will give us pigeons by the dozen. It will be quite easy to get to the nests if we let ourselves down with a rope.'

'Agreed!' exclaimed Gordon. 'Suppose, Donagan, you go tomorrow?'

'That will suit me very well,' replied Donagan. 'Webb, Cross, and Wilcox, will you come too?'

'Rather!' They were only too pleased at the idea of blazing away into such a crowd of birds.

'But don't kill too many pigeons,' Briant told them. 'We know where to find them when we want them. Don't waste powder and shot—'

'All right!' Donagan did not like advice—particularly from Briant. 'It isn't the first time we've handled a gun.'

An hour later Moko announced that dinner was ready, and the boys hurried up the ladder on to the schooner and took their seats in the dining-saloon. As the vessel heeled over so much, the table sloped considerably; but that made little difference to those accustomed to the rolling of the ship. The shellfish, particularly the mussels, were declared excellent, although their seasoning left something to be desired; but at that age hunger is the best sauce. A biscuit, piece of corned beef with fresh water from the stream, taken when the tide was at the lowest so as to avoid its being brackish, made an acceptable meal.

The afternoon was spent in arranging the gear, Jenkins and his companions going off to fish in the river and having fair sport among the finny crowd swarming near its mouth. After supper all were glad to get to bed, except Baxter and Wilcox, whose turn it was to keep guard.

CHAPTER V

THE VIEW FROM THE CAPE

WAS IT an island, or a continent? That was the question preoccupying Briant, Gordon and Donagan, whose character and intelligence made them the leaders of this little world. Thinking of the future when the youngsters thought only of the present, they often talked together on the subject. Whether it was insular or continental, this land was evidently not in the tropics. That could be seen by the vegetation—oaks, beeches, birches, alders, pines, and firs. The country seemed to be nearer the southern pole than New Zealand, and, if so, a severe winter might be anticipated. Already a thick carpet of dead leaves covered the ground in the wood near the cliff; the pines and firs alone rettained their foliage.

'That's the reason' Gordon explained, 'the morning after the wreck I thought it best not to settle down permanently hereabouts.'

'That's what I think,' said Donagan. 'If we wait for the bad season, it will be too late to get to some inhabited part, for we may have to go hundreds of miles.'

'But we're only in the first half of March,' Briant protested.

'Well,' replied Donagan. 'The fine weather may last till the end of April, and in six weeks we might get well on the road—'

'If there is a road!'

'And why shouldn't there be?'

'Quite so,' said Gordon. 'But if there is, do you know where it leads to?'

'I know one thing,' retorted Donagan. 'It would be absurd not to leave the schooner before the cold rainy season, and to do that, we don't have to see nothing but difficulties at every step.'

'Better see them than start off like fools across a country we don't know anything about.'

'It's easy to call people fools when they don't think the same way you do.'

Donagan's comment might have led to a quarrel had not Gordon intervened.

'There's no good arguing. Let's understand each other. Donagan is right in saying that if we're near an inhabited country, we should get there without delay. But Briant says, are we near such a country? And there's no harm in that.'

'But, Gordon,' Donagan protested, 'if you go to the north or the south, or the east, you must get to somebody some time.'

'Yes, if we're on a continent,' replied Briant, 'and not on an island, maybe a desert island.'

'That's why we ought to find out,' said Gordon. 'To leave the schooner before we know whether there is or is not a sea to our east—'

'It's the schooner that will leave us,' Donagan reminded them. 'She can't last out the winter storms on this beach.'

Gordon agreed. 'But' he added 'before we venture into the interior we must know where we're going.'

'I'll go and reconnoitre,' Briant volunteered.

'So will I.' said Donagan.

'We'll all go,' Gordon decided, 'but we don't want to

THE VIEW FROM THE CAPE

drag the youngsters with us, and two or three of us will be enough.'

'It's a pity,' Briant commented, 'that there isn't any high hill to give us a good view. The land lies low, and even from the offing I couldn't see any elevation. The highest ground seems to be this cliff. Beyond it I suppose there's forests and plains, and marshes, with streams running through them.'

'We ought to have a look over the country before trying to get round the cliff where Briant and I couldn't find any cave.'

'Well, we'll try the north,' said Briant. 'If we can get up the cape at the far end, we might see a long way round.'

'That cape,' Gordon pointed out 'is two or three hundred feet high, and it ought to look right over the cliff.'

'I'll go,' Briant offered.

The bay ended in a huge pile of rocks, like a hill rising into a peak on the side nearest the sea. Along the curve of the beach it was seven or eight miles away, but in a bee-line, as the Americans say, it was probably not more than five, and Gordon had not over-estimated the height of the hill at three hundred feet above sea-level.

Was this high enough for a good view over the country? Might not the land to the eastward be shut in by high ground? But at least they could see whether or not the coast-line continued towards the north or not.

And so it was decided that the exploration should be made, and that the wreck should not be abandoned until the boys had found out whether they had been cast on an island or a continent, which could only be that of America. But no start could be made for the next five days, the weather having become misty and rainy; and until the wind freshened enough to blow the fog away, the view would not be worth the trouble of climbing.

The days were not lost. They were spent in work. Briant made it his duty to look after the younger boys, as if to watch over them with paternal affection were part of his nature. Thanks to his constant care, they were as well looked after as circumstances permitted. The weather was getting colder, and he made them put on warmer clothes from the stores found in the seamen's chests; this gave a good deal of tailoring work, in which the scissors were more in request than the needle, and Moko greatly distinguished himself. Costar, Dole, Jenkins and Iverson were elegantly attired in trousers and jerseys much too roomy for them, but reduced to a proper length of arm and leg.

The others did not stay idle. Under Garnett or Baxter, they were off among the rocks at low tide, gathering shellfish, or fishing with lines and nets at the mouth of the stream, amusing themselves to the general advantage. Busy in a way that pleased them, they hardly thought of their position, nor did they realise how serious it was. When they remembered their parents and friends, as they often did, they were sorrowful enough; but the idea that they would never see them again never occurred to them.

Gordon and Briant seldom left the wreck. Service was with them a good deal, and was always good-tempered and useful. He liked Briant, and had never joined Donagan's party, and Briant was not unmindful of his loyalty.

'This is first-rate,' he said. 'The schooner must have been dropped gently on the beach by some good fairy! There wasn't any such luck as this for Robinson Crusoe or the Swiss family.'

Young Jack grew stranger in his manner every day. Although he helped his brother in many ways, he rarely replied to a question, and he turned his eyes away whenever he was looked in the face. Briant was seriously uneasy at all this. As his senior by some four years, he had always had a good deal of influence over the boy, and ever since they had come on board he had noticed that Jack seemed like someone afflicted with remorse. Had he done anything that he dare not tell his brother? Several times Briant noticed that his eyes were red from crying. Was Jack going to be seriously ill? If so, how could they look after him? Here was trouble in store! And so Briant asked his brother quietly what was wrong with him.

'There's nothing the matter with me,' answered Jack. And that was all that could be got from him.

From March 11th to the 15th, Donagan, Wilcox, Webb, and Cross went shooting rock-pigeons. They always kept together, and it was clear that they wanted to form a clique apart from the rest. Gordon felt anxious about this; he saw that trouble must come of it, and he spoke about it, and tried to make the discontented ones understand how necessary union was for the good of the community. But Donagan replied to his advances so coldly that he thought it unreasonable to insist; yet he did not despair of destroying the germs of dissension which might have deplorable results, for events might help to bring about an understanding where advice had failed.

While the excursion to the north of the bay was stopped by misty weather, Donagan and his friends had plenty of sport. He was really an excellent shot, and he was very proud of his skill, and despised such contrivances as the traps, nets, and snares in which Wilcox delighted. Webb was a good hand with the gun, but did not pretend to equal Donagan. Cross had very little of the sportsman's sacred fire, and contented himself with praising his cousin's prowess. Fan, the dog, distinguished herself highly, and made no hesitation in jumping into the waves to retrieve the somewhat miscellaneous victims of the guns.

Moko refused to have anything to do with the cormorants, gulls, seamews, and grebes, but there were quite enough rock pigeons, as well as geese and ducks, to serve his purpose. The geese were of the bernicle kind, and from the direction they took when the report of the gun scared them away, it was to be supposed that they lived inland.

Donagan shot a few of those oyster-catchers which live on limpets, cockles, and mussels. There was in fact plenty of choice, although Moko found it no easy matter to get rid of the oily taste, and did not always succeed to the general satisfaction. But, as Gordon said, the boys need not be too particular, for the most must be made of the provisions on the ship.

On March 15th the weather appeared favourable for the excursion to the cape, which should settle the question as to island or continent. During the night the sky cleared of the mist which the calm of the preceding days had accumulated, and a land-breeze swept it away in a few hours. The sun's bright rays gilded the crest of the cliff. It looked as if that afternoon the eastern horizon would be clearly visible; and that was the horizon on which their hopes depended. If the line of water continued along it, this must be an island, and the only hope of rescue was from a ship.

The idea of visiting the end of the bay had first occurred to Briant, and he had decided to go off alone. He would gladly have been accompanied by Gordon, but he did not feel justified in leaving his companions without anyone to look after them.

On the evening of the 15th, finding the barometer remained steady, he told Gordon he would be off at dawn next morning. Ten or eleven miles, there and back, was nothing to a healthy lad who did not mind fatigue. The day would be enough for the journey, and he would be sure to get back before night.

Briant was off at daybreak without the others' knowing he had gone. His only weapons were a stick and a revolver, to be prepared for any wild beast that might come along, although Donagan had not come across any in his shooting expeditions. With these he also took one of the schooner's telescopes—a splendid instrument of great range and clearness of vision. In a bag hung at his belt he carried a little biscuit and salt meat, and a flask of brandy, in case any incident should delay his return.

Walking at a good pace, he followed the trend of the coast along the inner line of reefs, his road marked by a border of seaweed still wet with the retiring tide. In an hour he had passed the furthest point reached by Donagan in his foray after the rock pigeons. The birds had nothing to fear from him now; his object was to push on and reach the foot of the cape as soon as possible. The sky was clear of cloud, and if the mist returned in the afternoon, his journey might be useless.

During the first hour he kept on as fast as he could, and covered half his journey, and if no obstacle hindered him, he expected to reach the promontory by eight. But as the cliff ran nearer to the reefs, the beach became more difficult to traverse. The strip of land grew narrow, so that, instead of the firm path near the stream, he had to take to the slippery rocks, and make his way over viscous seaweed, and round deep pools and over loose pebbles where there was no safe footing. It was heavy going and took two full hours more than he expected.

'I must get to the cape before high water,' he reflected.

'The beach is covered by the tide, and the sea runs up to the foot of the cliff. If I have to turn to go back or to take refuge on some rock, I'll get there too late. I must get on at all cost before the tide comes in.'

And the brave boy, trying to forget the fatigue which was beginning to creep over his limbs, struck out across what seemed the shortest way. Many times he had to take off his boots and stockings, and wade the pools, and now and then, for all his strength and activity, he could not avoid a fall.

It was here that the aquatic birds were in greatest number: swarms of pigeons, oyster-catchers, and wild ducks. A few seals were swimming among the breakers, but they showed no fear, and never attempted to dive. As they were completely unafraid, it looked as though many years had elapsed since men had come in chase of them. From this Briant concluded that the coast must be in a higher latitude than he had imagined, and some distance south of New Zealand. The yacht must have drifted to the southeast across the Pacific. And this was confirmed when Briant reached the foot of the promontory and found a flock of penguins which haunt only the Antarctic Ocean. They were strutting about in dozens, flapping their tiny wings, which they use not for flying but for swimming.

It was then ten o'clock. Exhausted and hungry, Briant thought it best to have something to eat before trying to climb the promontory, which raised its crest some three hundred feet above the sea. He sat down on a rock out of reach of the rising tide, which had begun to cover the outer ridge of reefs. An hour later he would not have been able to pass along the foot of the cliff without running the risk of being trapped by the flood. But there was nothing to be

THE VIEW FROM THE CAPE

anxious about now, and in the afternoon the ebb would leave the way dry.

While the food satisfied his hunger, the halt rested his back and limbs. Alone, and far from his companions, he coolly considered the situation, resolving to do his best for the good of all. Then he thought of his brother Jack, whose health was causing him much anxiety. He felt that Jack must have done something serious—probably before his departure—and he decided to question him so closely that he would have to confess. For an hour Briant sat thinking and resting. Then he closed his bag, threw it over his shoulder, and began to climb the rocks.

The cape ended in a narrow ridge, and its geology was remarkable. It was a mass of metamorphic rock, detached from the cliff, and differing from it completely in structure, the cliff consisting of layers of a chalky material, like those bordering the English Channel.

Briant noticed that a narrow gorge cut the promontory off from the cliff, and that the beach extended northwards out of sight. But the promontory, being at least a hundred feet higher than the neighbouring heights, would give him a good view.

The ascent was not easy. He had to climb from one rock to another, some being so large that he could barely reach them. But as he belonged to that order of boys we classify as climbers, and brought all his powers into play, he eventually reached the top.

With his glass he first looked to the east. As far as he could see the country was flat. The cliff was its greatest elevation, and the ground gently sloped towards the interior. In the distance were a few hillocks hardly worth mentioning. There was much forest land, and under the yellow foliage rose many streams that ran towards the coast. The surface was level as far as the horizon, which might be a dozen miles away. It did not look as though the sea were there.

To the north Briant could make out the beach running straight away for seven or eight miles; beyond was another cape, and a stretch of sand that looked like a huge desert. To the south was a wide marsh. He had surveyed the whole sweep of the westerly horizon.

Was he on an island or a continent? He could not say. If it were an island, it was a large one. That was all he could ascertain.

The he looked westward. The sea was shining under the oblique rays of the sun, which was slowly sinking.

Suddenly he raised his glasses and looked out into the offing.

'Ships!' he exclaimed. 'Ships going past!'

Three black spots appeared about fifteen miles away on the circle of gleaming waters.

Great was his excitement. Was he the sport of some illusion? Were they really vessels that he could see?

He lowered the glass and cleaned the eyepiece, which had clouded with his breath. He looked again.

The three points seemed like ships with nothing visible but their hulls. There was no sign of their masts, and no smoke to show that they were under way.

And then he reflected that they were too far off for his signals to be seen; and as it was unlikely that his companions had seen these ships, the best thing he could do was to get back to the wreck and light a big fire on the beach. And then—when the sun went down—he kept his eye on the three black spots. One thing was certain, they did not move.

Again he looked through the glasses and for some

minutes he kept them in the field of his objective. Then he saw that they were three small islands that the schooner must have passed near to when they were hidden in the mist.

It was two o'clock. The tide began to retire, leaving the line of reefs bare at the foot of the cliff. Briant, thinking it was time to return to the wreck, made ready to descend the hill.

But once again he looked eastward. Now that the sun was lower, he might see something that had hitherto escaped him. And he did not regret doing so; for beyond the forest he could now see a bluish line, which stretched from north to south for many miles, its two ends lost behind the confused mass of trees.

'What's that?' he wondered.

And again he looked.

'The sea! Yes! The sea!'

And the glass almost fell from his hands.

It was the sea to the eastward, there could be no doubt about that! It was not a continent they were cast up on, it was an island. An island in the immensity of the Pacific, which they could not possibly leave!

And then all the perils that surrounded him appeared before his mind as in a vision. His heart almost stopped beating, but, struggling against the involuntary weakness, he resolved to do his best to the last, however threatening the future might be.

A quarter of an hour later he had regained the beach; by the same way as he had come in the morning he returned to the wreck. He reached it about five and found his comrades impatiently awaiting his return.

CHAPTER VI

A SPELL OF RAIN

THAT EVENING after supper, Briant told the older boys the result of his exploration. To the east, beyond the forest zone, he had distinctly seen a line of water extending from north to south. That this was the sea horizon was beyond all doubt. Hence it was not on a continent that the yacht had been wrecked, it was on an island.

Gordon and the others received the information with great excitement. What! They were on an island with no means of leaving it! Their plan to find a road eastward would have to be abandoned! They would have to wait till a ship came in sight! Could this really be their only chance of rescue?

'But mightn't Briant be mistaken?' asked Donagan.

'Haven't you mistaken a cloud-bank for the sea?' asked Cross.

'No,' answered Briant. 'I'm quite certain I've made no mistake. What I say was a line of water, and it formed the horizon.'

'How far off was it?' asked Wilcox.

'About six miles from the cape.'

'And beyond that,' Webb inquired, 'weren't there any mountains, any high ground?'

'No! Nothing but the sky.'

Briant was so positive that it was unreasonable to retain the least doubt.

But Donagan, as always when he argued with Briant,

was still obstinate. 'And I repeat that Briant has made a mistake. And until we've seen it with our own eyes—'

'Which we shall do,' asserted Gordon, 'for we must know the truth.'

'And I say we haven't a day to lose,' Baxter protested, 'if we're to leave this place before the bad weather, supposing we're on a continent.'

'We'll go tomorrow, if the weather permits,' Gordon decided. 'We'll start on an expedition that may last some days. I say weather permitting, for to plunge into the forest in bad weather would be madness—'

'Agreed, Gordon,' Briant answered. 'And when we reach the other side of the island—'

'If it is an island?' interrupted Donagan.

'But it is one!' Briant declared impatiently. 'I haven't made any mistake. I distinctly saw the sea in the east. It pleases Donagan to contradict me, as usual—'

'And you aren't infallible, Briant!'

'No, I am not! But this time I'm right! I'll go myself to this sea, and if Donagan likes to come with me—'

'Certainly I shall go.'

'And so shall we,' chimed in three or four of the bigger boys.

'Good!' Gordon agreed. 'But don't get excited, my dear young friends! If we're only boys, we may as well act like men. Our position is serious, and any rashness may make it worse. We mustn't all go into this forest. The youngsters can't come with us, and we cannot leave them all on the wreck. Donagan and Briant may go, and two others may go with them—'

'I'll go!' declared Wilcox.

'So will I!' said Service.

'Very well,' Gordon agreed. 'Four is quite enough. If

you're too long coming back we can send a few others to your rescue, while the rest remain with the schooner. Don't forget that this is our camp, our house, our home, and we can only leave it when we're sure that we're on a continent.'

'We're on an island,' Briant repeated, 'For the last time I say so!'

'That we shall see!' replied Donagan.

Gordon's sensible advice had had its effect in calming the discord. Obviously—and Briant saw it clearly enough —it was advisable to push through the central forest and reach the water. If it were a sea to the eastward, there might be other islands beyond a channel they could cross; and if they were on an island of an archipelago, surely it was better to know it before taking steps on which their safety might depend. It was certain that as far as New Zealand there was no land to the west. The only chance of reaching an inhabited country was to journey towards the sun.

But it would not be wise to attempt such an expedition except in fine weather. As Gordon had just pointed out, it would not do to behave like children, they must act like men. In the circumstances in which they were placed, with the future so threatening, if the intelligence of these boys did not develop quickly, if the levity and inconsistency natural at their age carried them away, or if disunion were allowed amongst them, the position would become critical. And it was for this reason that Gordon resolved to do everything to maintain order amongst his comrades.

However eager Donagan and Briant might be to start, a change of the weather made them wait. A cold rain had fallen since the morning and the fall of the barometer indicated a period of squally weather, whose duration it was impossible to predict. It would have been too risky to venture out under such circumstances.

But was this to be regretted? Assuredly not. That all were in a hurry to know if the sea surrounded them may be imagined. But even if they were sure of being on a continent, were they likely to venture into a country they knew nothing about, and that when the rainy season was coming on? Suppose the journey were to extend to hundreds of miles, could they bear the fatigue? Would even the strongest among them reach the end? No! To carry out such an expedition with success, it must be put off till the days were long, and the harshness of winter overpast. And so they would have to content themselves with spending the rainy season at the wreck.

Gordon had meanwhile been trying to find out in what part of the ocean they had been wrecked. His atlas contained a series of maps of the Pacific. In tracing the course from Auckland to the American coast he found that the nearest islands passed to the north were the Society Islands, Easter Island, and the island of Juan Fernandez, on which Selkirk—a real Crusoe—had passed so much of his life. To the south there was not an island up to the boundary of the Antarctic Ocean. To the east there were only the Archipelagoes of the Chiloe Islands and Madre de Dios, along the coast of Patagonia, and lower down were those about the Straits of Magellan and Tierra del Fuego, which are lashed by the terrible seas round Cape Horn.

If the schooner had been cast on one of these uninhabited islands off the Patagonian pampas, there would be hundreds of miles to be traversed to reach Chile or the Argentine Republic. And the boys would have to act with great circumspection if they were not to perish miserably in crossing the unknown.

So thought Gordon. Briant and Baxter looked at the matter in the same way. And doubtless Donagan and the others would end by agreeing with them.

The scheme of exploring the eastern coast was not given up, but during the next fortnight it was impossible to put it into execution. The weather was abominable, nothing but rain from morning to night, as well as violent squalls. The way through the forest would have been impracticable; and the expedition had to be postponed, notwithstanding the keen desire to unravel the mystery of continent or island.

During these stormy days the boys remained at the wreck, but they were not idle. They were constantly at work making good the damage done to the yacht by the weather, for owing to the wet the planks began to give, and the deck ceased to be water-tight. In places the rain would come in through the joints where the caulking had been torn away, and this had to be made good at once. Repairs were also needed to stop not only the water-ways, but the air-ways opened in the hull. Gordon would have used some of the spare sails for the purpose, but he could not bring himself to sacrifice the thick canvas which might come in so usefully for tents, and so he did the best he could with tarpaulins.

Besides this, there was the urgent question of finding a better shelter. Even if they did go eastward, they could not move for five or six months, and the schooner would not last as long as that. And if they had to abandon her in the rainy season, where were they to find a refuge? The cliff, on its western face, had not the slightest indentation that could be utilized. It was on the other side, where it was sheltered from the wind from the sea, that search must be made, and, if necessary, a house built large enough to hold them all.

Meanwhile the cargo was done up into bales and packages, all duly numbered and entered in Gordon's pocket-book, so that when it became necessary they could be quickly carried away under the trees.

Whenever the weather was fine for a few hours, Donagan, Wilcox, and Webb went off after the pigeons, which Moko more or less successfully cooked in different ways. Garnett, Service, Cross, and the youngsters, including Jack when his brother insisted on it, went fishing. Among the shoals of fishes that haunted the weeds on the reef were hake of large size, and among the fronds of the huge seaweed, some of which were four hundred feet long, was a prodigious quantity of small fish that could be caught by hand.

It was a treat to hear the exclamations of the youthful fishers as they drew their nets or lines to the edge of the reef.

' I've got a lot! I've such a splendid lot! ' exclaimed Jenkins. ' Oh! they're big ones! '

' So are mine! Mine are bigger than yours! ' shouted Iverson, calling on Dole to help him.

' They'll get away! ' exclaimed Costar, as he ran up to help.

' Hold on! Hold on! ' Garnett adjured them, going from one to the other. ' Get in your net quickly.'

' But I can't! ' wailed Costar, as the net was dragging him in.

And then with a united effort the nets were got in on the sand. It was time, for in the clear water there was a number of ferocious lampreys, which would have made short work of the fish caught in the meshes; but although many

A SPELL OF RAIN

were lost in this way, enough were saved to furnish the table. A good deal of hake were caught, and found to be excellent, either fresh or salted. The fish at the river mouth were chiefly a kind of gudgeon, which Moko found he could best cook fried.

On the 27th of March a more important capture promised a somewhat amusing adventure.

When the rain left off in the afternoon, the youngsters started off to fish in the river.

Suddenly there were loud shouts from them—shouts of joy, it is true—but also shouts for help.

Gordon, Briant, Service, and Moko, who were busy on the schooner, dropped their work, ran off to help, and soon cleared the five or six hundred yards to the stream.

'Come along!' shouted Jenkins.

'Come and see Costar and his charger!' said Iverson.

'Quick, Briant, quick! or he'll get away!' shouted Jenkins.

'Let me get down! Let me get down! I'm afraid,' Costar implored them, gesticulating in despair.

'Gee up!' yelled Dole, who was with Costar on some moving object.

This was a turtle of huge size, one of those enormous chelonians usually found floating on the surface of the sea. This time it had been surprised on the beach, and was seeking to regain its natural element.

In vain the boys, who had slipped a cord round its neck, were trying to keep the animal back. It kept moving off with irresistible strength, dragging the whole band behind it. For a lark Jenkins had perched Costar on the carapace, with Dole astride behind him; and the youngster began to scream with fright as the turtle slowly neared the water.

'Hold on! Hold on, Costar!' shouted Gordon.

'Take care your horse doesn't get the bit between his teeth!' Service warned him.

Briant could not help laughing; for there was no danger. As soon as Dole let go, Costar had only to slip off to be safe.

But it was advisable to catch the animal; and if Briant and the others united their efforts to those of the little ones, they might stop him; and they must put a stopper on his progress before he reached the water, where he would be safe.

The revolvers Gordon and Briant had brought with them from the schooner were useless, for the shell of a turtle is bullet-proof; and if they attacked him with the axe, he would draw in his head and paddles, and be unassailable.

'There is only one way,' said Gordon; 'we must turn him over!'

'And how?' asked Service. 'He must weigh at least three hundredweight and we can never—'

'Get some spars! Get some spars!' shouted Briant. And, followed by Moko, he ran to the schooner.

The turtle was now not more than thirty yards from the sea. Gordon soon had Costar and Dole off its back, and then, seizing the cord, they all pulled as hard as they could, without in the least stopping the advance of the animal, which could have dragged all Charman's school behind it.

Luckily, Briant and Moko returned before the turtle reached the sea.

Two spars were then run underneath it, and with a great effort it was pitched over on its back. Then it was a prisoner, for it could not turn over on to its feet. And just as it was drawing in its head Briant gave it such a crack with the hatchet that it died almost immediately.

'Well, Costar, are you still afraid of this big brute?' asked Briant.

'No! No! Briant, for now he's dead.'

'Good!' Service declared, 'But you daren't eat him!'

'Can you eat him?'

'Certainly.'

'Then I'll eat him, if he's good,' Costar licked his lips at the thought.

'It is good stuff,' Moko rightly declared that turtle meat was quite a dainty.

As they could not think of carrying away the turtle as a whole, they had to cut it up where it was. This was not very pleasant, but the boys had begun to get used to the disagreeable necessities of Crusoe life. The most difficult thing was to break into the carapace, as its metallic hardness turned the edge of the axe; they succeeded at last in driving a cold chisel in between the plates. Then the meat, cut away in pieces, was carried to the schooner. And that day the boys had an opportunity of convincing themselves that turtle soup was exquisite, to say nothing of the grilled flesh which Service had unfortunately let burn a little over too fierce a fire. Even Fan showed in his own way that the rest of the animal was not despised by the canine race.

The turtle yielded over fifty pounds of meat—a great saving to the stores of the yacht.

In this way March ended. During the three weeks since the wreck all the boys had done their best preparing for a long stay on this part of the coast. Before the winter set in there remained to be settled this important question of continent or island.

On 1st April, the weather gave signs of changing. The barometer rose slowly, and the wind began to moderate.

There were unmistakable symptoms of an approaching calm of perhaps longish duration.

The bigger boys discussed the matter, and began to prepare for an expedition whose importance was obvious to all.

'I don't think there'll be anything to stop us tomorrow,' said Donagan.

'Nothing, I hope,' agreed Briant. 'We ought to be ready to get away early.'

'I understand,' Gordon asked 'that the line of water you saw in the east was six or seven miles from the cape.'

Yes, but as the bay is a deep curve, it's possible that the sea may be much nearer here.'

'Then,' continued Gordon, 'you won't be away more than twenty-four hours?'

'That is, if we can go due east. But can we find a way through the forest when we've got round this cliff?'

'Oh! that won't stop us!' Donagan declared.

'Perhaps not,' said Briant, 'but there may be other obstacles—a watercourse, a marsh, who knows? It will be best, I think, to take rations for some days.'

'Quite so, and let it be understood that if we're not back in two days you needn't be anxious.'

'I shall be anxious if you are away more than half a day,' said Gordon. 'But that isn't the question. As the expedition has been decided on, let it proceed. You have not only to reach this eastern sea, but to reconnoitre the country behind the cliff. This side we have found no cave, and when we leave the schooner we shall have to carry the things where they'll be sheltered from the sea breeze. To spend the rainy season on this beach seems impracticable.'

'You're quite right, Gordon,' answered Briant, 'and we'll look out for some place where we can settle down.'

'At least, until we have found that we can't get out of this so-called island,' Donagan still kept returning to his idea.

'That's understood,' said Gordon, 'although the season is already rather advanced. At any rate, we'll act for the best. So tomorrow you start!'

Preparations were soon finished. Four days' provisions were stowed in bags carried over the shoulders, four guns, four revolvers, two boarding-axes, a pocket compass, a powerful telescope, and the usual pocket utensils, matches and tinder-box, seemed enough for a short expedition that was not without its dangers. Briant and Donagan, and Service and Wilcox, who were to go with them, were cautioned to be careful not to push forward without extreme circumspection, and never to separate. Gordon could not help feeling that he would have done better not to keep Briant and Donagan together. But it was best for him to remain at the wreck, so as to look after the younger boys. So he took Briant apart, and made him promise to avoid any subject that might cause a quarrel or disagreement.

The barometrical prognostics were realized. Before nightfall the last clouds had vanished in the west. The line of sky and sea met in a clear horizon. The magnificent constellations of the southern hemisphere sparkled in the firmament, the Southern Cross conspicuously pointing to the Antarctic Pole.

On the eve of their separation Gordon and his comrades were sad at heart. And as their eyes sought the sky, there came to them the thought of the fathers and mothers and friends and country that they might never see again.

CHAPTER VII

THE EXPLORERS

AT SEVEN in the morning, Briant, Donagan, Wilcox, and Service left the wreck. The sun rising in a cloudless sky gave promise of one of those pleasant October days almost peculiar to the temperate zone of the northern hemisphere. Neither the heat nor the cold would be excessive. If any obstacle should be met with that would delay or stop the advance, it would be due entirely to the nature of the ground.

The young explorers set out obliquely across the beach to reach the foot of the cliff. Gordon had advised them to take Fan with them; her instinct might be very useful; and so the dog formed part of the expedition.

A quarter of an hour after their start, the boys had disappeared under the trees. The birds were in numbers, but as no time was to be lost, Donagan had the good sense to restrain his love of shooting. And Fan, realising that useless runnings to and fro were not advisable, kept near her masters without diverging to the left or right more than her duties as scout required.

The plan was to skirt the base of the cliff until the cape at the north of the bay was reached and then to strike off for the sheet of water Briant had seen. This was not the shortest way, but it was the safest, and a mile or two extra was not much for healthy boys who were such good walkers.

When they reached the cliff, Briant recognised the place where he and Gordon had been on their first exploration.

As there was no way in this part of the limestone wall to the south, a pass must be looked for towards the north, even if they went all the way to the cape. To do this would take a day, but no other way was open if there were no road through the cliff on its eastern face. Briant explained this to his companions, and Donagan, after vainly endeavouring to climb up the slope, made no objection.

They kept on for an hour, and as there could be no doubt they would have to go all the way to the cape, Briant was anxious about the route's being clear. Would not the tide be up over the beach when they got there? That would mean the loss of half a day waiting till the water left the reef bare.

'Let's hurry on,' he suggested, after pointing out the importance of reaching the reef before the tide came in.

'Bah!' answered Wilcox. 'We're not afraid of wetting our ankles.'

'Your ankles, and perhaps your body, and perhaps even your ears!' replied Briant. 'The tide rises five or six feet at the least. We'd better keep straight for the cape.'

'You're guide, Briant,' Donagan reminded him, 'If we're behindhand it'll be your fault.'

'Then don't let's lose any time. Where's Service?' And he shouted 'Service! Service!'

The boy was not in sight. He had gone off with his friend Fan, and had just disappeared behind an angle of the cliff, a hundred yards off to the right.

But as if in answer there was a shout, and the dog was heard to bark. Was Service in danger, then?

In a minute Briant, Donagan, and Wilcox reached their companion, who had stopped before a partial fall of the cliff—a fall of ancient date. Owing to infiltration, or the action of the weather in wearing away the limestone, a sort of half-funnel had been formed from the top of the wall to the ground, with the point below. In the wall a gorge had been opened with the sides at a slope of from forty to fifty degrees, and the irregularities formed a series of points on which it would be easy to find a footing. Active boys like these could easily scramble up to the top, unless a new fall took place to stop them.

Although it was risky they did not hesitate.

Donagan was the first to begin to mount the heap of stones at the base.

'Wait! Wait!' shouted Briant. 'There's no use being rash.'

But Donagan did not hear, and as he thought it was necessary for his reputation to get in front of his companions—and especially of Briant—he was soon half-way up the gorge.

His companions followed his example, taking care not to get immediately under him, so as not to be hit by the fragments he dislodged, and which came rolling down to the ground. All went well, and Donagan had the satisfaction of reaching the crest of the cliff before the others.

Already he had drawn his glasses from their case, and was scrutinising the forests that stretched out of sight towards the east.

There was the same panorama of verdure and sky as Briant had seen from the summit of the cape, though not so extended, for the cliff was some hundred feet lower.

'Well?' asked Wilcox. 'Can't you see anything?'

'Nothing!' answered Donagan.

'Let me have a look,' Wilcox suggested.

Donagan held out the glasses to his companion, not without obvious satisfaction.

'I don't see the least line of water,' agreed Wilcox, lowering the glasses.

'That's good enough,' Donagan asserted, 'to prove there isn't any. You can look, Briant, and I think you'll admit your mistake.'

'I don't care,' answered Briant. 'I know I haven't made any mistake.'

'That's rather strong!'

'Not a bit of it! The cliff is lower than the cape, and the range of view is less. If we were as high as I was, the blue line would be seen six or seven miles off. You'd soon see it where I did, and you'd see it's impossible to mistake it for a cloud-bank.'

'It's easy to say that,' said Wilcox.

'And just as easy to prove,' answered Briant. 'Let's cross this flat and get through the forest and keep on till we get there.'

'That's good,' sneered Donagan. 'We shall have to go rather far, and I'm not sure it's worth the trouble.'

'Stay here then, Donagan,' Briant retorted, 'Service and I will go on alone.'

'We'll go too,' said Wilcox. 'Come on, Donagan!'

'Not till we've had something to eat,' protested Service.

The need for this was acknowledged, and after half an hour the march was resumed.

The first mile was soon covered. The grassy soil presented no obstacle. Here and there a few mosses and lichens covered the rocky mounds. An occasional clump of shrubs dotted the ground, a few tree-ferns or club mosses, heaths, hollies, or clumps of berberis with leathery leaves that flourish even in the highest latitudes.

When Briant and his comrades had crossed the upper plateau, they found the descent on the other side of the cliff as high and perpendicular as that towards the sea. Had it not been for the bed of a half-dry torrent down which they made their way with difficulty, they would have had to keep on up to the cape.

When the forest was reached, the road became more difficult. Fallen trees obstructed the path, and the underwood was so thick that it had sometimes to be cut through. The boys had to use their axes like the pioneers through the forests of the New World, and this meant a halt almost every minute. Arms got more tired than legs, and because of the delay not more than three or four miles had been accomplished when evening began to close in.

It certainly seemed as though no human beings had ever been through this forest. At any rate they had left no trace of their passage. The trees had been felled, not by the hand of man, but by storms or old age. Here and there through the thicket were signs of the recent passage of some small-sized animals, and these were caught sight of occasionally, without its being possible to recognise the species.

Donagan's hand often itched to seize his gun and fire at these timorous quadrupeds. Briant had only to intervene to prevent his companions committing the imprudence of revealing their presence by the report. But although Donagan realised he had to keep his favourite weapon silent, he had to be spoken to pretty often. At every step flew up partridges with very delicate flesh, or the birds known as martinettes, besides thrushes, wild geese, and grouse, and numbers of others that could have been knocked down in hundreds. If the boys had to stop in this place, the gun would procure them abundant food. This Donagan could not but admit, as he resolved to make up later on for the reserve now imposed upon him.

The forest chiefly consisted of birch and beech trees,

which developed their tender green foliage up to a hundred feet from the ground. Among the other trees were well-grown cypresses, myrtaceae with reddish wood, and magnificent groups of 'winters' with their bark throwing off an aroma like that of cinnamon.

At two o'clock a second halt was made in a little clearing, through which ran a shallow stream—such a stream as would have been called a creek in North America. Its waters were perfectly limpid and flowed gently over the bed of blackish rocks. To look at its peaceful shallow current, cumbered with no deadwood or drifting bushes, no one could believe that its rise was far away. Nothing was easier than to cross it by the stones scattered in its bed, but in one place some flat stones lay so symmetrically as to attract attention.

'That's queer!' said Donagan.

It looked as though a causeway had been laid from bank to bank.

'You might call it a dike!' Service commented as he began to cross it.

'Wait! Wait!' Briant warned him. 'We must have a look at these stones.'

'They couldn't have put themselves there,' Wilcox pointed out.

'No,' Briant agreed. 'It looks as though someone had been making a path across the stream. Let's get nearer!'

They examined every stone of this strange pathway, which projected only a few inches above the stream, and would be covered in the rainy season. But could they be sure that the hand of man had put these stones in the creek? No! It was more likely that they had been brought down by the floods, and gradually piled up to form the dike; this was the explanation adopted by Briant and his companion after a careful examination.

Neither the left nor right bank showed traces of footsteps, and there was nothing to prove that man had ever set foot on the gap in the forest.

The creek flowed away towards the north-east. Did it then throw itself into the sea which Briant declared he had seen from the cape?

'At least,' Donagan suggested, 'it may be the tributary of some river which flows towards the west.'

'We'll see in time,' Briant did not care to reopen the discussion. 'But so long as it runs to the east we may as well follow it, if it doesn't wind too much.'

Crossing the creek by the dike, the four boys set out. It was easy to follow the bank, except here and there where a clump of trees ran their roots down into the water, while their branches met overhead and extended from bank to bank. Although the creek made a bend now and then, yet its general direction was shown by the compass to be eastwards. But its mouth ought to be a long way off, for the stream did not gain in quickness nor did its bed become wider.

About half-past five Briant and Donagan were forced to agree that the creek had turned towards the north, so that to follow it would take them too much out of their way. So they had to abandon it, and to plunge eastward under the thick foliage of beech and birch.

At times the underwood was so high that in order not to lose one another they had to keep up a constant shouting.

They had been walking all day and there was nothing to indicate the proximity of a sheet of water. Briant began to get anxious. Had he been the sport of an illusion when he descried the horizon from the summit of the cape?

'No! No!' he repeated to himself. 'I can't have been mistaken! I can't be! It isn't so!'

It was now seven in the evening and the edge of the forest had not been reached. Darkness was coming on: it would soon be too dark to move.

It was decided to halt and pass the night beneath the shelter of the trees. With a good slice of corned beef there was no chance of starving; with warm coverings they need not fear the cold. Besides, they might light a fire with some dead branches, if the precaution, excellent as it might be against animals, might not attract such natives as might be prowling about.

'Better not run the risk of being seen,' Donagan reminded them.

All agreed to this; and only supper was thought about. There was no lack of appetite, and after making a deep hole in the rations they had brought with them, they were about to make themselves comfortable at the foot of a gigantic birch when Service pointed out a thicket a few yards off. From it rose a moderately-sized tree whose lower branches bent till they touched the ground. There, on a heap of dry leaves, the four boys lay down and wrapped themselves well up. At their age sleep is not long in coming, and they were soon soundly off, while Fan, left to guard them, copied their example.

Once or twice, however, the dog heard a prolonged growl. Evidently there were some animals, tame or wild, prowling in the forest; but they did not come near the camp.

It was nearly seven when Briant and the others awoke. The oblique rays of the sun, piercing the thick mass of leafage, dimly lit up the place where they had passed the night.

Service was the first to go out of the thicket. Immediately he began to shout—'Briant! Donagan! Wilcox! Come here!'

'What's the matter?' asked Wilcox, who always had to say something. 'Service, you frightened us.'

'All the better!' answered Service. 'Look here! See where we've been sleeping!'

It was not a thicket at all. It was a cabin made of leaves, one of those huts the Indians call 'ajoupas,' formed by interlacing branches. The ajoupa was very old, for the roof and walls were held up only by the tree; and its style was the same as that in use among the natives of South America.

'Then there are inhabitants?' wondered Donagan, casting a rapid glance around him.

'Or at least there have been,' said Briant, 'for this hut couldn't have made itself.'

'That explains the causeway across the creek,' Wilcox pointed out.

'Well,' Service added, 'if there are inhabitants, they're very good fellows to build this hut expressly for our use.'

In reality nothing was less certain than that these natives were 'good fellows.' Clearly they frequented, or had frequented, this part of the forest at some period more or less remote. But they might be Indians if the land were joined to the continent, or Polynesians, or even cannibals, if it were an island of one of the archipelagoes of Oceania. If so, the danger was great, and more than ever it was important to solve the problem.

Briant was starting off when Donagan proposed that they should carefully examine this hut, which seemed to have been abandoned for a long time. They might find some utensil or instrument or tool whose origin they could recognise.

The heap of dry leaves was carefully pulled over, and in one corner Service found a fragment of burnt clay which might have been a bowl or a cup—just a trace of the work of man but that was all.

They therefore set out, and by half-past seven had started, compass in hand, bearing due east, the ground sloping gradually as they went. For two hours they kept on, slowly, very slowly, through dense thickets of shrubs and small trees, and once or twice having to cut their way through with the axe.

A little before ten o'clock they caught sight through the trees of a horizon. Beyond the forest was a wide plain dotted with mastic trees, thyme bushes, and clumps of heath. Half a mile to the eastward it was bounded by a strip of sand, on which beat the surf of the sea, which extended right up to the horizon.

Donagan said nothing. He was angry to find that his companion had not made a mistake.

And Briant said nothing. He did not wish to triumph over his friend.

Telescope at his eye, he looked all round.

On the north the shore, now brightly lit by the sun's rays, seemed to curve off to the left. At the south it was the same, but the curve was sharper.

There could no longer be any doubt. It was not a continent, it was an island on which the schooner had been wrecked, and all hope would have to be given up of getting away from it except through outside help.

Beyond, there was no other land in sight. It seemed as though the island lay lost by itself in the immensity of the Pacific.

The four boys crossed the plain to the beach and halted at the foot of a sandhill, meaning to have lunch and then to go back through the forest. If they made haste they might get back to the wreck before nightfall.

The meal was not a cheerful one. Hardly a word did they exchange.

At length Donagan picked up his bag and his gun, and said—'Let's be off!'

And all four, giving a last look at the sea, were making a move, when Fan ran off along the beach.

'Fan! Here! Fan!' shouted Service.

But the dog continued to caper along the wet sand and at last she rushed into the sea, and began to drink.

'She's drinking!' exclaimed Donagan.

And in an instant he was by the side of the sea and drinking the water that Fan so much enjoyed.

It was fresh! It was a lake stretching away to the eastern horizon. It was not the sea!

CHAPTER VIII

THE CAVE

AND SO the important question on which the safety of the boys depended was still unsolved. That the supposed sea was a lake there could be no doubt. But might not the lake be on an island? If the exploration were continued, would not a sea be discovered beyond—a sea there was no way of crossing?

The lake was of considerable size, for it touched the horizon on three of its sides, as Donagan pointed out, and it was certainly more likely to be on a continent than on an island.

'Then it must be America on which we've been wrecked,' Briant commented.

'I always thought so,' said Donagan, 'and it seems I wasn't wrong.'

'Anyhow,' Briant pointed out, 'it was a line of water I saw to the east.'

'Yes, but it wasn't the sea.'

Donagan's self-satisfaction was obvious from this reply, which showed more vanity than good-nature. Briant said no more. For the common welfare it was better that he had been mistaken. On a continent they would not be imprisoned as they would on an island. But they would have to wait for a favourable time before setting out towards the east. The difficulties experienced in reaching the lake were as nothing to what might be expected by the whole party on a much longer journey. And it was already the beginning of April, and the southern winter comes earlier than the northern. There could be no thought of setting out before the return of the fine weather.

But the position would soon be untenable in the bay, exposed as it was to the winds, and before the end of the month the schooner would have to be abandoned. If no cavern could be found in the cliffs, would the boys be better off here by the lake? Wouldn't it be as well to explore its neighbourhood more carefully? The exploration would delay their return for a day or two, and would give Gordon some anxiety, but Briant and Donagan did not hesitate. Their provisions would last another day, and there was no sign of a change of weather. So it was decided to go south by the side of the lake.

There was another motive for the exploration's being extended.

Undoubtedly the district had been inhabited or rather frequented by man. The causeway in the creek and the hut were clear indications of human presence at a period more or less recent, and yielded evidence it was advisable to confirm before moving to new quarters for the winter. Perhaps other evidence might be found? If savages had not been here, some shipwrecked sailor might have stayed for a time, until he started on his way inland. It was well worth while exploring the district bordering on the lake.

There was only one question to settle. Should Briant and Donagan go south or north? But as to go southwards was to move nearer the wreck, that direction was decided on. It would be seen later on if it were advisable to go to the end of the lake.

It was about half-past eight when the four boys began their march, skirting the grassy sandhills that diversified the plain, bounded on the west by the masses of greenery.

THE CAVE

Fan hunted about in front and put up several flocks of birds that hastened to shelter under the bushes and ferns. Here and there rose clumps of a sort of red and white cranberry, and plants of wild celery. But the guns had to be kept silent, for the environs of the lake were possibly visited by savages.

In following the shore, sometimes at the foot of the sandhills, sometimes along the sand, the boys easily covered a dozen miles during the day. They found no trace of savages. No smoke rose from the trees. No footprints marked the sand, wet with the sheet of water that stretched away into the offing. Not a sail was to be seen on the horizon, not a boat on the surface. The lake was deserted. If the country had been inhabited, it did not seem to be so now.

Wild beasts there were none. Several times during the afternoon a few birds appeared on the edge of the forest, but it was impossible to get at them.

Service exclaimed: 'They're ostriches.'

'Very small ostriches, then,' Donagan answered, 'for they aren't too tall.'

'If they are ostriches,' said Briant, 'and if we're on a continent—'

'Do you still doubt it?' asked Donagan ironically.

'It must be the American continent, where such animals are very abundant,' continued Briant, 'that's all I wanted to say.'

About seven in the evening, a halt was called. Next day, unless something happened, the journey would be continued to the wreck. That evening it was not possible to go further. At the halting-place one of the rivers flowed out from the lake, and this would have to be crossed by swimming. Darkness was setting in and the country could be but imperfectly seen, but there seemed to be a cliff on the right bank of the watercourse.

Briant, Donagan, Wilcox and Service, after supper had been despatched, thought only of a night's rest, under the stars this time, no hut being discoverable. And the stars were bright and sparkled brilliantly, and the crescent moon moved slowly down to set in the Pacific. All was quiet on the lake and on the beach. The four lads, nestled between the enormous roots of a beech-tree, slept so soundly that even a thunderstorm would not have awakened them.

Like Fan, they failed to hear sounds close by, which might have been the cry of a jackal, or the more distant growling which was probably that of wild beasts. In these countries where ostriches live wild, they might expect the jaguar and cougar, the tiger and lion of South America. But the night passed without incident.

About four in the morning, just as the dawn was showing on the horizon above the lake, the dog began to give signs of uneasiness, growling gently, and sniffing the ground as if she wanted to be sent off in search of something.

It was nearly seven when Briant awoke his comrades. All were up immediately, and while Service nibbled a bit of biscuit, the others went to take a look round the country beyond the watercourse.

'Well,' exclaimed Wilcox, 'it's a good thing we didn't try to cross the water yesterday. We should have stuck in the marsh.'

'Yes,' Briant agreed, 'it's marsh, and it stretches right away to the south, and we can't see the end of it.'

'Just look at the ducks,' added Donagan, 'and teal and

THE CAVE

snipe on it! If we could take up our quarters here for the winter, we shouldn't want for game.'

'And why shouldn't we?' asked Briant, walking towards the right bank of the stream.

Behind it was a lofty cliff which ended in a peak. Its two sides joined at an angle; one ran by the bank of the river, the other skirted the lake. Was this cliff the one which shut in the bay where the schooner was wrecked? That could not be verified until a more complete exploration of the district had been made.

The right bank of the river was about twenty feet high and ran along the base of the cliff; the left bank was very low, and could scarcely be distinguished from the pools and bogs of the marshy plain which extended out of sight towards the south. To make out the direction of the river they would have to climb the cliff, and this Briant decided to do before starting for the wreck.

The first thing was to look round the outlet of the stream from the lake. This was only about forty feet across, but as it increased in width, so also it increased in depth.

'Just look here!' said Wilcox, as he reached the end of the cliff.

A pile of stones had attracted his attention, forming a sort of dam, similar to the one they had seen in the forest.

'There's no doubt this time,' said Briant.

'No! No doubt at all,' remarked Donagan, pointing to some pieces of wood at the end of the dike.

The remains were obviously those of a boat of some sort. One piece, half rotten and covered with moss, and curved like a stem, held an iron ring eaten away with rust.

'A ring! A ring!' exclaimed Service.

And the four stood still, looking around as if the man

who had used the boat and built the dike were about to appear.

But nobody came! Many years had evidently gone by since the boat had been left to rot by the side of the stream, and the man had rejoined his fellows or ended his miserable existence on this land he could never leave; and it may well be understood how the boys felt at this clear evidence of human habitation and the thoughts it gave rise to.

Meanwhile Fan had been behaving strangely, as if she had at last got on a scent. Her ears were pricked up, her tail wagged, and her nose was held close to the ground, as she worried about under the bushes.

'Look at Fan,' exclaimed Service.

'She can smell something,' said Donagan, stepping towards her.

Fan had just stopped with one paw raised and neck stretched out. Then she suddenly rushed towards a clump of trees at the foot of the cliff by the side of the lake.

Briant and his comrades followed her. A few minutes later they stopped before an old beech on whose bark were cut two letters and a date:

F. B.
1807

The boys would have stood silent and motionless for some time before this inscription if Fan had not run back round the angle of the cliff.

'Here, Fan! Here!' shouted Briant.

The dog did not return, but her noisy barking reached them.

'Take care,' Briant warned them. 'Don't separate, and keep on your guard.'

Indeed they could not be too careful. A band of savages might be in the neighbourhood, and their presence was to be feared rather than wished for, if they were those Indians who infest the pampas of South America.

The guns were cocked, and the revolvers got out ready as the boys advanced round the angle of the cliff, and up the narrow bank of the stream. They had not taken a dozen paces before Donagan stooped to pick up something from the ground. It was a pickaxe with the handle half rotten—a pickaxe of American or European origin, not one of those heavy tools made by the Polynesian savages. Like the ring on the boat, it was deeply rusted, and must have been left behind many years ago.

At the foot of the cliff were traces of tillage, a few irregular furrows, a little square of yams, which, left to themselves, had run wild.

Suddenly a mournful bark was heard, and Fan reappeared, seized with some inexplicable agitation. She turned round, ran in front of her masters, looked back at them, called them, and seemed to invite them to follow.

'There's certainly something extraordinary the matter,' Briant tried in vain to get the dog quiet.

'Let's go where she's taking us,' Donagan signed to Wilcox and Service to follow.

Ten yards further on Fan stopped before a mass of brushwood and bushes, which reached up to the very foot of the cliff.

Briant looked to see if the bushes hid the corpse of some animal, or even of a man on whose traces Fan had fallen. Clearing away the bushes, he saw a narrow opening.

'Is there a cave here?' he exclaimed, stepping back a few paces.

'Likely enough,' said Donagan. 'But what's in the cave?'

'We'll see,' answered Briant.

And with his hatchet he began to cut away the entanglement about the entrance. He listened, but could hear no suspicious noise.

Service was about to slip through into the cave, when Briant stopped him.

'See what Fan is going to do first.'

The dog barked angrily, twice or thrice, in a way that was anything but reassuring for the occupant of the cave, had one been there.

What did it mean? The boys had to find out. Briant put a handful of dry twigs across the opening and lighted them to see if the air were foul. The twigs crackled and burnt brilliantly; evidently the air was breathable.

'Shall we go in?' asked Wilcox.

'Yes,' Donagan answered.

'Wait till we can see our way,' put in Briant. And, cutting a resinous branch from one of the pine-trees close by, he lighted it. Then, followed by his companions, he stepped into the cave.

The opening was about four feet high and two feet wide; but it at once grew larger, forming a cavity twelve feet high and twice as wide, with a floor of hard dry sand.

As he hurried on, Wilcox stumbled over a wooden bench, near a table on which were some domestic utensils: a stoneware jug, some large shells that had been used as plates, a knife with a notched and rusty blade, two or three fish-hooks, and a tin cup, empty like the jug. Near the opposite wall was a sort of box, made of planks roughly nailed together, and containing a few tattered clothes.

There could be no doubt that the excavation had been inhabited. But when, and by whom? What had become of the human being who had once lived here?

At the end was a miserable pallet covered with some fragment of linen. At the head, on a bench, was a second cup and a wooden candlestick, with only a burnt match on the bowl.

The boys recoiled from the pallet, at first thinking it might hold a corpse.

Repressing his repugnance, Briant lifted up the covering.

The pallet was empty.

A minute later the boys, who were deeply touched, had rejoined Fan, who was still keeping up her mournful barking.

They descended the bank of the stream for about twenty yards, and suddenly stopped. A feeling of horror nailed them to the spot.

There, among the roots of a beech tree, were the remains of a skeleton.

And so to this place there had come to die the unhappy man who had lived on this land, and the cave that had been his dwelling-place had not become his tomb.

CHAPTER IX

FRANÇOIS BAUDOIN

THE BOYS were silent. Who was this man who had come here to die? Was he a shipwrecked sailor to whom no help had come in his last hour? To what nation did he belong? Was he young when he arrived in this corner of the earth? Was he an old man when he died? How had he supplied his wants? If he had been shipwrecked, had any others survived with him? And if so, had he remained alone after the death of his companions in misfortune? Did the various things in the cave belong to his ship, or had he made them with his own hands? But to such questioning no answer might ever be given.

And here was something more serious! If it was on a continent that this man had found refuge, why had he not reached some town in the interior or some port on the shore? Were there such difficulties, such obstacles to his getting back to his own country, that he could not overcome them? Was the distance so great that he thought he could not accomplish it? Clearly he had fallen down, weak from sickness or old age, and had not had strength enough to regain the cave, but had died at the foot of the tree! And if the means of safety to the north and east had failed him, why should they not fail these boys from the wreck of the schooner?

It was important to examine the cave with the greatest care. Who knew if they might not find a document which might throw some light on this man, or his birth-place, or the length of the stay! And on the other hand it was advisable to ascertain if they could take up their quarters here for the winter after leaving the wreck.

'Come on!' said Briant.

And, followed by Fan, they entered the cave by the light of another resinous torch.

One of the first things they saw was a shelf fixed against the right wall; on this was a bundle of clumsy candles made of fat and tow. Service lighted one of these candles and placed it in the wooden candlestick, and the search began.

In the first place the shape of the cave was noticed: there was no doubt that it was quite suitable to live in. It was a large cavern, dating back from geological times. There was no trace of damp, although the only ventilation was through the one opening on to the bank of the stream. The walls were as dry as if they were granite, without any trace of the drops of moisture which in some caves crystallize and form stalactites. Its position sheltered it from the sea breezes. Daylight came in but little, it is true, but opening one or two windows in the wall would ventilate it enough for fifteen people.

Its dimensions—twenty feet by thirty feet—made it too small to be used at the same time as dormitory, refectory, general store, and kitchen. But it would only be required for five or six months, after which a start could be made to the north-east for some town of Bolivia or the Argentine Republic. If they had to take up their permanent abode here, the cave would obviously have to be made larger by digging into the friable limestone. But as it was it would do very well till the summer season.

This being ascertained, Briant made a careful list of the things it contained. These were not many. The unfortunate man had been almost destitute. What had he secured from the wreck? Nothing but odds and ends, broken spars, pieces of plank that he had made up into the pallet, the table, the box, and the benches, which formed the only furniture. Less favoured than the survivors of the schooner, he had not had a workshop ready at hand. A few tools, a pickaxe, an axe, two or three cooking utensils, a little cask of brandy, a hammer, two cold chisels, a saw—these were all. They had doubtless been saved in the boat whose remains lay near the dike.

So thought Briant, and so he told his companions. And then the feeling of horror at the sight of the skeleton, and the thought that they might die in the same way, gave place to a feeling of confidence at their possession of so many things which this man had lacked.

But who was he? Where was he born? When was he wrecked? No doubt many years had passed since his death: the state of the bones found at the foot of the tree showed that only too well! Besides, there was the rust on the pickaxe and the ring, the thicket of bushes at the entrance of the cave, all tending to show that he must have died years ago. Would any new discovery change this hypothesis into a certainty?

The search was continued. A few other objects were brought to light—a second knife with the blades broken, a pair of compasses, a kettle, an iron ring, a marline-spike. But there was no nautical instrument, no telescope, no mariner's compass, not even a musket.

As the man had to live, it seemed as though he must have snared his food instead of shooting it. But an explanation of the difficulty offered itself when Wilcox exclaimed: 'What's that?'

'That?' inquired Service.

'He's been playing bowls?' said Wilcox.

'Bowls?' asked Briant in surprise. But in a moment he recognised the use of the two round stones which Wilcox had picked up. They formed one of those implements known as the bolas, which consists of two balls tied together with a cord, and is used by the South American Indians. When a skilful hand throws the bolas, the cord encircles the limbs of the animal, and for a moment entraps it so that it falls an easy prey to the hunter.

The inhabitant of the cave had made this bolas, as well as a lasso, a long loop of leather used at shorter distances.

But who was this man? Was he an officer or an ordinary seaman who had put his reading to profit! It would be difficult to ascertain this unless something further were discovered.

At the head of the bed, under a rag that Briant had thrown aside, Wilcox found a watch hung on a nail fixed in the wall.

This watch was not a common watch such as sailors usually wear, but was of finer workmanship, and had a double case of silver and a silver key and chain.

'The time! The time!' said Service.

'The time won't tell you anything,' said Briant. 'The watch probably stopped days before the unfortunate man died.'

Briant opened the case, not without difficulty, for the hinges were rusty, and saw that the hands pointed to twenty-seven minutes past three.

'But,' said Donagan, 'the watch has the maker's name. That might tell us—'

'You're quite right,' Briant agreed.

And looking inside the case, he managed to read these words engraved on the plate—

'Delpeuch, Saint Malo.'

The name of the maker and his address.

'Then he was French!' exclaimed Briant.

There seemed little doubt that a Frenchman had lived in this cavern until death put an end to his misery.

To this proof another was soon added when Donagan, who had turned over the pallet, found a note-book with its yellow pages covered with pencil writing.

Unfortunately most of the writing was illegible. A few words could, however, be deciphered, and among others were—François Baudoin, whose initials were the same as those the man had cut on the tree. The note-book was the daily journal of his life from the day he had been cast ashore. And in the fragments of phrases that time had not entirely effaced Briant managed to read *Duguay-Trouin,* evidently the name of the ship that had been lost in this distant corner of the Pacific.

At the beginning was a date, 1807—the same as that which had been cut under the initials on the tree.

It was, then, fifty-three years since François Baudoin had been thrown on this coast; and since his shipwreck he had received no help from outside. If he had not moved to some other place on the continent, was it because the obstacles were insurmountable?

More than ever the boys thought of the gravity of their situation. How could they do what this man had not done, a man accustomed to hard work and broken to fatigue?

Another discovery was to show them that all attempts to leave the country would be in vain.

As Donagan turned over the note-book he found a folded paper between the leaves. It was a map, drawn in ink made probably of soot and water.

'A map!' he exclaimed.

'Which François Baudoin has drawn with his own hand!' said Briant.

'If that is so,' Wilcox pointed out, 'the man couldn't be an ordinary seaman but one of the officers of the *Duguay-Trouin.* To make a map of this place—'

'And that's what it is,' broke in Donagan.

There could be no mistake. At the first glance the boys recognised the bay where they had been wrecked, the bank of reefs, the beach on which they had encamped, the lake they had skirted on the western side, the three islands in the offing, the cliff running along to the stream, and the forests covering the central region.

Beyond the opposite bank of the lake were other forests extending to yet another shore, and that shore was washed by the sea on all sides!

There was an end to all the plans of going eastward to seek safety! And so Briant was right after all, and Donagan was wrong! The sea surrounded the imaginary continent on every side. It was an island and that was why François Baudoin had not been able to leave it.

It was easy to see that the map was correct. The distances were probably mere estimates based on the times taken to traverse them, and not arrived at by triangulation; but to judge by what was already known, the errors could not be important.

It was clear that the shipwrecked man had been all over the island, that he had noted the chief geographical details and that the hut and the causeway at the creek were probably of his construction.

As François Baudoin showed it, the island was oblong,

and resembled an enormous butterfly with open wings. In the centre of the forest was the lake, eighteen miles long and five wide, large enough to account for the boys' not being able to see its distant shores and mistaking it for the sea. Many streams ran out of this lake, and notably the one in front of the cave, which entered the bay close to the camp.

The only height of importance in the island was the cliff up to the cape on the north. The southern part was shown by the map to be arid and sandy, while beyond the stream was an immense marsh which narrowed to a point as it ran to the south. In the north-east and south-east were long lines of sandhills, which gave this part of the coast a very different aspect from that of the bay in which the schooner was wrecked.

According to the scale at the foot of the map the island was about fifty miles long from north to south, and twenty-five wide from east to west. Reckoning the irregularities of its shape, it was 150 miles in circumference. But there was no knowing to which of the Polynesian group it belonged, or if it lay by itself in the Pacific. One thing was certain, that the boys would have to stay on it; there was no getting away. And as the cave afforded an excellent refuge, it was best to bring all their goods across to it before the storms had broken up the schooner.

At present the best thing to be done was to return to the camp without delay. Gordon would be getting anxious: three days had elapsed since Briant and his comrades left him, and he would be fearing that some misfortune had happened to them.

Briant suggested that they should start that very day at eleven. There was no good in climbing the cliff, as the map showed the shortest way was to follow the right bank of the river to the bay, which ran from east to west. At the most this would be about seven miles, and take but a few hours.

But before leaving, the boys paid the last mark of respect to the shipwrecked Frenchman. With the pickaxe they dug a grave at the foot of the tree on which François Baudoin had cut his initials, and a wooden cross marked the spot.

This pious ceremony over, they returned to the cave, and closed the entrance, so that no animals could get in. Then, having finished what was left of their provisions, they started along the right bank of the stream by the base of the cliff. In an hour they reached the spot where the high ground trended off to the northwest. Along the river the road was easy, for the bank was clear of shrubs and trees.

As they walked, Briant took careful note of the river, bearing in mind that it ran from the lake into the bay. It seemed to him that on the upper part of its course at least a boat or raft might be towed or poled along, and this would make the transport of the goods easy, especially if advantage were taken of the tide, which ran up into the lake. In its course there were no rapids, and no narrows or shallows to make it unnavigable. For the first three miles after it left the lake, everything seemed to favour his plan.

But about four in the afternoon, the road by the bank had to be abandoned. The stream ran into a wide marsh which could not be crossed without risk, and the boys thought it best to take to the forest.

Compass in hand, Briant led the way to the northeast, so as to reach the bay by the shortest road. But considerable delay was produced by the closeness of the thickets;

and under the dense shade of the birches, pines, and beeches, darkness fell at the sun set.

Two miles were accomplished in this tiring manner. After getting round the marsh, which stretched a long way to the north, the best plan would undoubtedly have been to return to the river bank, but this would have added so much to the length of the journey that Briant and Donagan decided it was not worth the loss of time. So they kept on through the forest until about seven when they discovered that they had somehow gone astray.

Would they have to pass the night under the trees? They might have done this pretty comfortably had not all the provisions been exhausted.

'Come on!' said Briant, 'if we keep to the west, we must reach the camp.'

'Unless the map is wrong,' commented Donagan, 'and that wasn't the stream which runs into the bay.'

'Why should the map be wrong, Donagan?'

'And why shouldn't it be, Briant?'

Evidently Donagan had not yet got over his annoyance at being proved wrong, and was prepared to throw doubt on Baudoin's statements. Why, was not clear, for as far as the boys had gone the map had proved to be fairly correct.

Briant saw no advantage in disputing the matter, and strode off to the west.

At eight the night had become so dark that it was impossible to see ahead; and the end of the forest seemed as far off as ever.

Suddenly through a gap in the trees a bright light shot through the air.

'What is that?' asked Service.

'Probably a meteorite,' said Wilcox.

'No. It was a rocket!' answered Briant.

'A rocket from the schooner!'

'Then it must be a signal!' exclaimed Donagan, firing his gun in answer.

Soon a second rocket sped through the darkness. Briant and his companions made for it, and three-quarters of an hour later they reached the schooner.

CHAPTER X

THE RAFT

THE RECEPTION the explorers met with can be imagined. Gordon, Cross, Baxter, Garnett and Webb gripped their hands, while the younger boys threw their arms around their necks and shouted for joy. Fan took part in the rejoicing, and barked as loudly as the youngsters cheered. It seemed so long since Briant and his companions had gone away!

'Had they been lost? Had they fallen among savages? Had they been attacked by cannibals?' Such were the questions those who stayed in camp had been asking.

But Briant, Donagan, Wilcox and Service had now returned to tell them the story of their expedition. As, however, they were very tired after their long day's work, the story was postponed till the morning.

'We're on an island!'

That was all Briant said, and that was enough to reveal the troubles in store for them, although Gordon received the news without betraying much discouragement.

'Good! I'll wait,' he seemed to be saying to himself, 'and I'll not trouble myself about it till it comes.'

Next morning—5th April—all the three boys and also Moko, whose advice was always valuable, met in the bow of the yacht, while the others were still asleep. Briant and Donagan told their comrades all that had happened: how a causeway across a stream, and the remains of a hut, had led them to believe that the country was inhabited. They explained how the wide sheet of water they had at first taken for the sea was nothing but a lake; how fresh traces they had come upon had led them to the cave, where the stream flowed out of the lake; how the bones of François Baudoin had been discovered; and how the map he had made showed that it was an island on which the schooner had been wrecked.

The story was told in full, and now all who looked at the map understood only too well that help could come only from the sea.

However, if the future presented itself in the gloomiest colours, and the boys could place their hope only in God, there was one who felt much less alarmed than the others, and that was Gordon. The young American had no relatives in New Zealand. And to his practical, methodical, organising mind, there was nothing so very difficult in the task of founding a colony. He saw the chance to use his natural gifts, and he did not hesitate to keep up the spirits of his comrades by promising them a supportable existence if only they would help him.

And in the first place, as the island was of considerable size, it seemed impossible that it was not marked on the map of the Pacific near the American coast. They turned to the atlas, but no island of importance could they find outside the archipelagoes, which include the Fuegian or Magellanic Islands, and those of Desolation, Queen Adelaid, Clarence, and so forth. If it had been in one of these archipelagoes and separated from the continent only by narrow channels, Baudoin would certainly have shown it on his map, and this he had not done. It must be an isolated island, and probably more north or south than these archipelagoes. But without the necessary instruments it was impossible to fix its position.

All that could be done at present was to take up their quarters and make themselves comfortable before the wet season made it impossible to move.

'The best thing to do,' said Briant, 'is to move into the cave near the lake. It would make a capital place to live in.'

'Is it large enough to hold the lot of us?' asked Baxter.

'No,' answered Donagan, 'but I think we could make it larger by digging out another cave from it. We have tools—'

'Let's try it first as it is,' suggested Gordon, 'and if it's too small we can—'

'And let's get there as soon as we can,' interrupted Briant.

The matter was urgent. As Gordon had said, the schooner became less habitable every day. The late rains and the hot sun had opened up the cracks in the hull and deck, and the torn sails had allowed the wind and water to find their way inside. The sand on which it rested had been undermined, and it had heeled over and sunk deeper into the sand. If a storm were to come, there was every chance of the wreck's going to pieces in a few hours. The sooner the boys cleared out the better, and it would be well for them to take the hull to pieces methodically, to secure all that would be useful, such as beams, planks, iron, copper, with a view to properly fitting up 'French Den,' as the cave had been called in memory of the shipwrecked Frenchman.

'And in the meantime where shall we live?' asked Donagan.

'In a tent,' answered. 'In a tent under the trees by the riverside.'

'That's the best thing,' Briant agreed, 'and let's begin without losing an hour.'

The demolition of the yacht, the unloading of the material and provisions, the construction of a raft for the transport of the cargo, would take at least a month of hard work, and before they left the bay it would be the first week of May, which corresponds to the first week in November in the northern hemisphere, the beginning of winter.

Gordon had chosen the bank of the river as the site of the tent because the transport was to take place by water. No other way was more direct or convenient. To carry all that remained of the yacht through the forest or along the bank of the river would have been almost impossible; but by taking advantage of the tide a raft could be got up the river without much trouble.

In its upper course, as Briant had found, the stream contained no obstacle such as falls, rapids, or bars. An expedition to reconnoitre its lower course from the swamp to the mouth was made in the yawl; and Briant and Moko assured themselves that the river was navigable in that stretch also. There was thus an unbroken line of communication between the bay and French Den.

The days that followed were employed in arranging the camp at the side of the river. The lower branches of two beeches were joined by long spars to the branches of a third, and were used to hold up the yacht's spare mainsail, which fell down on each side to the ground. Into this tent, which was firmly stayed and strutted, they transported the bedding and furniture, the weapons and ammunition, and the bales of provisions. As the raft was to be built of the timbers of the yacht, they had to wait till they had demolished the wreck before they began to build it.

There was nothing to complain of in the weather, which continued dry. When there was a wind, it came from the land, and the work went on uninterruptedly.

By 15th April there remained on the schooner only such things as were too heavy to move until she broke up—among them the lead used for ballast, the water-tanks in the hold, the windlass, and the galley, which were too heavy to be taken away without apparatus. The spars and rigging, shrouds, and stays, chains, anchors, ropes, hawsers, lines, yarns, and so forth, were gradually removed to the ground near the tent.

Busy as they were with this work, the wants of each day were not neglected. Donagan, Webb, and Wilcox devoted a few hours to shooting the rock pigeons and the birds frequenting the marsh. The youngsters went searching for molluscs when the tide left the reef bare. It was pleasant to see Jenkins, Iverson, Dole, and Costar hunting about in the pools like a lot of ducklings, and sometimes getting their legs wet and being scolded by the severe Gordon, and excused by the gentler Briant. Jack also went out with the youngsters, but he never joined in their shouts of laughter.

Things went on satisfactorily and methodically, thanks to Gordon, whose common sense was seldom at fault. Even Donagan gave in to him when he would not give in to Briant or any one else. And harmony reigned in the little world.

But there was need of haste. The second fortnight of April was not so fine. The average temperature fell, and during the early morning the thermometric column fell below freezing. The winter was coming, and with it would come its retinue of hail and snow and storm.

The boys began to clothe themselves more warmly, to put on the thick jerseys and jackets. To find them was easy enough, for they were all down in Gordon's notebook, arranged in qualities and sizes. The youngest boys were Briant's special care. He saw that they did not get their feet cold or dawdle in the cold air when they were out for a swim; at any suggestion of a cold in their heads he made them sleep near the fire, which he kept in night and day; and often he kept Dole and Costar in the tent, while Moko gave them gruel and physic from the schooner's medicine-chest.

When the schooner had been emptied of all its contents, the hull, which had broken apart in many places, was attacked. The sheets of copper sheathing were taken off very carefully. Then the pincers, and crowbars, and hammers were brought into play to rip off the planks which the nails and trenails fastened to the frame. This was a troublesome task for inexperienced hands and not very vigorous arms. And the breaking up went on very slowly until 25th April a storm came to help.

During the night, although they were already in the cold season, a thunderstorm occurred. The lightning played across the sky, and the rolling of the thunder lasted from midnight to sunrise, to the great terror of the smaller boys. It did not rain, fortunately, but several times the tent had to be supported against the fury of the wind. Owing to its being fixed to the trees it was still undamaged; not so the yacht, which lay directly exposed to the gusts from the offing and the full force of the waves.

The demolition was complete. The planks were torn off, the frame broken up, the keel smashed, and the whole thing reduced to wreckage. And there was nothing to complain of in this, for the waves as they retired carried

THE RAFT

off only a small portion of the wreck, which for the most part was kept back by the reef. The ironwork was easily picked up out of the sand, and all the boys set to work during the next day or so to collect it. The beams, planks, water-tanks, and so forth which had not been swept away lay scattered on the beach, and all that had to be done was to transport them to the right bank of the stream a few yards from the tent.

It was a heavy job, but in time it was done, though not without a good deal of fatigue. It was odd to see the boys all hanging on to a heavy piece of wood, hauling it along and encouraging each other with shouts. The heavier timbers were rolled on bits of round wood and levered along by spars. The most difficult things to move were the windlass, the galley stove, and the iron tanks, which were of considerable weight. If the boys had only had some practical man to guide them! If Briant had had his father, Garnett his, the engineer and the captain would have saved them from many mistakes they committed, and would commit again. Baxter, who was very intelligent in mechanical matters, displayed great cleverness and zeal; it was on his advice, supported by Moko, that tackles were fixed to piles driven into the sand, and thereby tenfold strength given to the boys, to enable them to finish their task.

In short, on the evening of the 28th, all that remained of the schooner had been taken to the place of embarkation; and without doubt the worst of the enterprise was over, for the river was to take the material up to French Den.

'Tomorrow,' said Gordon, 'we'll begin to build the raft.'

'Yes,' Baxter agreed, 'and to save any trouble in launching it, I propose building it in the river.'

'That won't be easy,' Donagan objected.

'Never mind,' replied Gordon, 'we'll try. If it gives us more trouble to get together, it won't trouble us at all to get it afloat.'

No doubt this was the best way; and next morning they began the framework of the raft, which was to be large enough to take a heavy crowded cargo.

The beams from the schooner, the keel broken in two pieces, the foremast, what remained of the mainmast broken off three feet above the deck, the rails, and the midship beam, the bowsprit, the fore-yard, the main-boom and the gaff, had been taken to a part of the river beach which the water covered only at high tide. The boys waited till the tide rose, and then the wood was brought out into the stream. There the largest pieces were placed side by side, and bound together, with the others placed crossways upon them.

In this way a solid framework was obtained, about thirty feet long and fifteen feet wide. All day long the boys worked hard at the raft, and by nightfall the framework was complete. Briant then took care to lash it to the trees on the bank, so that the rising tide could not carry it up stream, or the ebb take it out to sea. Then everyone, thoroughly tired out after such a laborious day, sat down to supper with a formidable appetite, and slept soundly till the morning.

At dawn they again set to work. A platform had now to be built on the framework. The deck planks and strakes of the schooner's hull now came into use. Nails driven in with heavy hammer-strokes, and ropes passed over and under, fastened everything firmly together.

Working at their hardest, this took three days, although there was not an hour to lose. A little ice had already appeared on the surface of the pools among the reefs and along the edge of the stream. The shelter of the tent became insufficient in spite of the fire. Sleeping close to each other, covered with the thickest wraps, Gordon and his companions found it difficult to put up with the cold. Hence the necessity of pushing on with getting ready to take up their quarters in the cave, where they hoped to defy the winter, which in these latitudes is very severe.

The deck had been fixed as firmly as possible, so that it should not be displaced on the voyage; for that meant that the cargo would be swallowed up in the bed of the stream; and to avoid such catastrophe it was better to delay the departure for a day.

'However,' said Briant, 'we mustn't hang about beyond the sixth of May.'

'Why not?' asked Gordon.

'Because the day after tomorrow is new moon, and the tides will be higher for a few days after that. The higher they are, the easier we shall get up the river. Just think what a fix we shall be in if we have to tow this heavy raft or pole it up! We could never do it against the current!'

'You're right,' replied Gordon. 'We must be off in three days at the latest.'

And all agreed to take no rest until the work was finished.

On 3rd May, they began to load the raft, being careful to trim it to keep it level. Everyone was occupied in this work according to his strength. Jenkins, Iverson, Dole, and Costar took charge of the lighter things, the utensils, tools, and instruments, and laid them on the deck, where Briant and Baxter stored them under Gordon's directions.

The bigger boys busied themselves about the heavier things, such as the stove, the water-tanks, the windlass, the ironwork, the sheathing, the rest of the schooner's ribs, the planking, the deckrails, and so forth. In the same way were brought on board the bales of provisions, the casks of wine, ale, and spirits, not forgetting several sacks of salt that had been found among the rocks. To assist in the loading, Baxter had erected two spars which were kept in position by four stays. To their end was fastened a tackle which enabled the material to be raised from the ground and lowered on to the raft.

All went on with so much prudence and zeal that in the afternoon of 5th May everything was in its place, and nothing remained but to cast off the raft's moorings. That would be done next morning at about eight, when the tide at the mouth of the stream began to rise.

The boys had doubtless imagined that, their task being over, they were to spend the rest of the day in taking things easy. They were to be disappointed, for Gordon made a suggestion which gave them something else to do.

'We're now going away from this bay,' he told them, 'and we shan't be able to look out over the sea, and if any ship comes in sight of the island, we shan't be able to signal to her. So it will be best, I think, to rig up a mast on the cliff, and hoist one of our flags and keep it flying. That ought to be enough to attract the attention of any ship that may pass within sight.'

The schooner's topmast, which had not been used in the raft, was accordingly dragged to the foot of the cliff where the slope by the riverbank was not too great, but it required much effort to get it up the rugged acclivity abutting against the ridge. Success came at last, however, and the mast was firmly fixed in the ground. Then with a halliard Baxter hoisted the British flag, and the same moment Donagan saluted it by firing his gun.

'Hallo!' Gordon commented to Briant. 'There's Donagan taking possession of the island in the name of Great Britain!'

'I'd be much astonished if it doesn't belong to Great Britain already,' said Briant.

Gordon's reply was a grimace, and by his always speaking of 'my island' he seemed to be claiming it for the United States.

Next morning at sunrise all were astir. The tent was taken down and the bedding carried on board the raft, with the sail over it to protect it from the weather. This, however, promised to be favourable enough, although a change in the direction of the wind had brought a good deal of mist in from the sea.

By seven everything was ready. The raft had been so loaded that it would accommodate them all for two or three days, and Moko had cooked enough food to last, so that no fire would be needed.

At half-past eight the boys gathered on the raft. The bigger ones, armed with poles and spars, took their places ready to steer it, for a rudder would have been no use in going with the stream.

A little before nine the tide began to make itself felt, and the framework began to creak and groan.

'Look out!' shouted Briant.

'Ready!' replied Baxter.

They were at the hawsers which moored the raft fore and aft to the riverbank.

'All ready!' agreed Donagan, who with Wilcox was in the front of the raft.

Soon the raft was afloat.

'Cast off!' Briant gave the order.

Away went the hawsers, and the heavily-loaded mass began to drift up stream, towing the yawl astern.

Every one was pleased when the raft began to move. If the boys had built a sea-going ship they could not have been more satisfied with themselves! And their little sentiment of vanity may well be forgiven!

The right bank of the river was bordered with trees, and higher than the left, which ran along by the marsh. Briant, Baxter, Donagan, Wilcox, and Moko used every effort to keep the raft away from the banks, for it would never do to run aground, but at the same time they did not cross the stream, for the tide was stronger along the right bank, whose height gave better holding to their poles.

Two hours after their departure they had floated about a mile. They had not grounded or run ashore. But according to Briant's estimate the river was quite six miles long, and as they could not hope to advance more than two miles with each tide, it would take them several tides to reach their destination.

In fact, about eleven the ebb began to run, and the boys had to bestir themselves to get the raft moored so that it did not drift back to the sea.

The raft could make a fresh start in the evening, but to venture with it then would be dangerous.

'I think it would be unwise,' Gordon explained. 'We should expose the raft to the chances of collision or grounding, and the shock might smash it up. I think we'd better wait till tomorrow, and go on with the day tide.'

The idea was too sensible not to meet with general approval. They might have to wait twenty-four hours, but

THE RAFT

the delay was preferable to risking the safety of the valuable cargo.

Half a day and the whole of the night were thus passed at the same place.

Donagan and his sporting friends, accompanied by Fan, were soon ashore on the riverbank.

Gordon advised them not to get far away, and they accepted his advice; and as they brought back two brace of fat bustards and a string of tinamous, their vanity was satisfied. Moko took charge of the game, to keep it for the first meal—breakfast, dinner, or supper—after reaching French Den.

During the day Donagan had seen no indication of the presence of man in the forest. He had, however, seen some tall birds running off, but he had failed to recognise them.

During the night Baxter, Webb, and Cross were on the look-out, ready if necessary to double the hawsers, or give them a little slack when the tide turned. All went well. Next morning, at a quarter to ten, the tide had risen high enough for the navigation to be resumed. The night had been cold, so was the day, and the sooner the raft reached its destination the better. What would the boys do if the river froze, or if an iceberg came down from the lake to enter the bay? Here was something to think about, something they did not cease to worry over till they reached French Den.

But it was impossible to go quicker than the flood-tide, impossible to go against the stream when the tide failed, impossible to advance more than a mile in an hour and a half. They covered half of their journey. About one in the afternoon a halt was made at the swamp which Briant had had to go round in returning to the wreck, and advantage was taken of the halt to explore the part adjoining the river. For a mile and a half Moko, Donagan, and Wilcox rowed away in the yawl to the north, and stopped only when the water became too shallow. The swamp was a prolongation of the marsh which extended along the left bank; it seemed very rich in water-fowl, and Donagan was able to shoot a few snipe to add to the larder.

The night was very still and cold, with a quiet biting breeze that almost died away as it crossed the river valley. Ice formed in the stream, but only in thin flakes, which broke or melted at the slightest shock. In spite of every effort to keep warm, no one was comfortable on the raft. Among the youngsters, Jenkins, and Iverson were in a very bad humour, and complained bitterly at having had to leave the schooner; and Briant had to take them in hand and talk them to sleep.

At length, in the afternoon of the next day, with the aid of the tide, which lasted till half-past three in the afternoon, the raft arrived in sight of the lake and was run aground in front of the entrance to French Den.

CHAPTER XI

A CAPTURE

THE LANDING took place amid shouts of joy from the youngsters, to whom any change from the ordinary life was as good as a new game. Dole capered about on the bank; Iverson and Jenkins ran to the side of the lake; Costar took Moko aside and asked him: 'Didn't you promise us a good dinner?'

'Yes, but you'll have to do without that,' said Moko.

'And why?'

'Because I shan't have time to get dinner today.'

'What! No dinner?'

'No, but there'll be supper. And the bustards will be just as good for supper!'

And Moko grinned and showed his white teeth.

The youngster gave him a punch in token of goodwill, and ran off to join his friends, whom Briant had warned not to get out of sight.

'Haven't you gone with them?' he asked his brother.

'No! I'd rather stop here!' Jack answered.

'You'd much better take a little exercise,' said Briant. 'I'm not at all easy about you, Jack. You've got something you're hiding from me. Are you ill?'

'No! There's nothing the matter with me.'

Always the same reply, which never satisfied Briant, who was resolved to clear the matter up some day, even at the cost of a scene with the obstinate boy.

But there was no time to lose if the night were to be spent in French Den.

At the outset the cave had to be visited by those who did not already know it. And as soon as the raft was securely moored to the bank in a backwater away from the current, Briant asked his friends to go with him. Moko had taken one of the ship's lamps, whose flame, greatly increased by the lenses, gave a remarkably bright light.

First the boys had to clear away the entrance. As the branches had been placed by Briant and Donagan, so were they found: and so no human being, no animal, had tried to enter the cave.

After the boughs were cleared away the boys crept through the narrow entrance. In the glare of the lantern the cave was much better lit than by the resinous torches of the shipwrecked man's candles.

'Eh! We shall find this a tight fit,' Baxter had begun to measure the cave.

'Bah!' exclaimed Garnett. 'If we put the beds one over the other as they do on board ship—'

'Why?' asked Wilcox. 'We've only got to put them side by side on the ground—'

'And then,' said Webb, 'we shan't have any room to move about.'

'Well,' Briant told him, 'you won't move about, that's all. Have you a better place to offer us, Webb?'

'No—but—'

'But,' broke in Service, 'the important thing is to have a place to shelter us. I don't suppose Webb imagined he'd find a complete mansion—with drawing-room, bedroom, hall, smoking-room, bathroom—'

'No, of course not,' said Cross. 'But is there any place where you can cook?'

'Yes. Outside,' replied Moko.

'That will be very inconvenient in bad weather,' Briant pointed out. 'I thought we should bring the stove inside tomorrow—'

'Cooking in the cave, where we eat, where we sleep!' Donagan exclaimed in a tone of unmistakable disgust.

'Well, you can use your smelling-salts, Lord Donagan!' exclaimed Service, laughing loudly.

'I will if I want to, Mr. Cook's Mate!' Donagan frowned.

'All right! All right!' Gordon reminded them. 'Whether the thing is nice or not, we'll have to decide about it at once! If the stove is used for cooking, it will also do to keep us warm. As to getting some room by digging out chambers in the rock, we shall have all the winter for that, if it can be done. But now let's take French Den as it is, and get into it as soon as possible.'

The beds were brought in and laid in order on the sand. Close as they were, the boys, accustomed to the small cabin of the schooner, did not find them inconvenient.

This occupied the rest of the day. The large table from the yacht was placed in the middle of the cave, and Garnett and the youngsters laid the cloth.

Moko and Service had done their work well. A fireplace had been made between two large stones at the foot of the cliff, the fire being fed with dry wood gathered by Webb and Wilcox under the trees. About six o'clock the soup—the meat biscuit which had only to be boiled for a few minutes—was giving forth a pleasing fragrance; a dozen tinamous, spitted on an iron bar, were roasting before a brisk fire over a dripping-pan, into which Costar would very much have liked to put his fingers; and while

Dole and Iverson acted as turnspits, Fan followed their movements with significant interest.

Before seven the boys were gathered round the table in the cave, which was their refectory and their dormitory. The benches, folding seats, and wicker chairs from the schooner had been brought in. The meal was substantial: hot soup, corned beef, roast tinamous, biscuit in place of bread, fresh water, with a taste of brandy, a little cheese, and a few glasses of sherry by way of dessert, made ample amends for the poor bill of fare they had had of late.

The day had been tiring. When hunger was satisfied the boys thought of little but going to sleep. But Gordon, moved by religious feelings, suggested that they should visit the tomb of Baudoin, whose dwelling they were now occupying. Night was darkening the horizon of the lake, and its waters were reflecting the last rays of the sun as they found the little mound and stood by the wooden cross.

By nine the beds were occupied, and all were asleep except Donagan and Wilcox, whose turn it was to watch, and who kept up a large fire at the mouth of the cave to scare away dangerous visitors.

The next day, 9th May, and the three days that followed, were spent by all hands in unloading the raft. Already the mist driven before the west wind announced a period of rain or snow. The temperature scarcely rose above freezing; and it was important that everything should be got into the cave as soon as possible.

For a few days, in view of the urgency of the work, the sportsmen stayed at home. In the afternoon, when Moko lighted his fire, he had the satisfaction of declaring that it worked admirably, so that even in bad weather food could be cooked.

During the following week Donagan, Webb, Wilcox, and Cross, together with Garnett and Service, had quite enough shooting to satisfy them. One day they had gone into the forest of birches and beeches by the side of the lake about half a mile from the cave. Here and there traces of the work of man were evident. Ditches were dug in the ground covered with a network of branches, they were too deep for animals falling into them to escape. But the state of these ditches showed that they had been made years ago, and one of them contained the remains of an animal which they failed to identify.

'Anyhow, they're the bones of a good-sized animal,' said Wilcox, who had slipped down into the ditch, and picked up the bones, now bleached by time.

'And it was a quadruped, for here are the bones of the four paws,' added Webb.

'Unless it was a five-footed animal,' Service objected 'and then it would be a show sheep or a phenomenal calf.'

'Always on the joke!' Cross grumbled.

'Well, we aren't forbidden to laugh,' answered Garnett.

'It's quite certain,' Donagan explained 'that the animal was a large one. Look at the size of its head, and its jaw and teeth. Service may amuse himself with his show calves and exhibition sheep, but if this animal came to life, he'd be in no mood to laugh.'

'Well hit,' Cross was always ready to approve of anything his cousin said.

'Do you think, then,' asked Webb of Donagan, 'that the animal was a carnivore?'

'Yes, there's no doubt of it.'

'A lion? A tiger?' Cross did not seem at all easy in his mind.

'If not a tiger or a lion,' Donagan replied, 'at least a jaguar or a cougar.'

'We must be on our guard,' said Webb.

'And not venture too far away,' Cross agreed.

'Do you hear, Fan?' Service spoke to the dog. 'There are big beasts here!'

Fan gave a cheery bark which certainly showed no anxiety.

The boys turned back to go to the cave.

'An idea,' said Wilcox. 'If you cover this ditch with fresh brushwood, we might catch something!'

'As you please, Wilcox,' said Donagan, 'though I'd rather shoot something in the open than massacre it at the bottom of a pit.'

Thus spoke the sportsman, but Wilcox, with his natural aptitude for devising snares, showed himself more practical, and began to put his idea into execution. His companions helped him cut some twigs from the neighbouring trees, and these were placed across the mouth of the pit so as to hide it completely. It was a rudimentary snare, no doubt, but such as is often used with success by the trappers of the Pampas.

To recognise the position of the pit, Wilcox broke off a few branches from the trees at the edge of the forest. Then they all returned to the cave.

These expeditions were not unproductive. Feathered and furred game abounded. Donagan tried to stalk some of them, but as they were difficult to get at, the consumption of powder and shot, much to the disgust of the sportsman, was not in proportion to the results. And this waste of ammunition evoked a few remarks from Gordon,

A CAPTURE

which were received by Donagan's friends with as ill a grace as by himself.

During one of these excursions a supply was collected of two useful plants which Briant had discovered on the first expedition to the lake. These were the wild celery, which grew in great abundance on the wet soil, and a cress, whose young shoots formed an excellent anti-scorbutic. These vegetables figured at all meals, being eaten for the sake of health.

As the cold had not yet frozen the surface of the lake and stream, a few trout were taken with the hook, besides a species of pike, very pleasant eating, providing the eater were not choked with the bones. One day Iverson returned triumphant, carrying a good-sized salmon which had nearly broken his line.

Meanwhile many visits had been paid to the pit: but no animal was taken, although a large piece of meat had been laid as a bait.

On 17th May, however, something did happen. Briant and a few others had gone off into the forest near the cliff, to see if there was any other cave close to French Den which might do as a store-house.

As they approached the pit, they heard a loud noise proceeding from it.

Briant struck off into the wood, and was soon joined by Donagan, who did not care to be behindhand. The others followed a few yards in the rear, with their guns at the ready, while Fan marched with her ears cocked and her tail stiff.

They were about twenty yards from the pit when the noise started again. In the middle of the branches was a hole through which some animal had fallen.

What the animal might be was not apparent, and the boys thought it best to be ready to defend themselves.

'Seize it, Fan, seize it!' said Donagan. And the dog ran off barking without any sign of fear.

Briant and Donagan ran towards the pit, and as soon as they had reached it they shouted 'Come here!'

'It isn't a jaguar?' asked Webb.

'Nor a cougar?' said Cross.

'No,' said Donagan, 'it's an ostrich!'

So it was, and the boys congratulated themselves that such birds frequented the forest, for their flesh is excellent—particularly in the fat part about the breast.

Although there was no doubt it was an ostrich, yet its mediocre size, its head like a goose's head, the coat of small plumes which enveloped its body like a greyish white fleece, showed that it belonged to the species of nandu, so numerous on the Pampas of South America. The nandu cannot be compared with the African ostrich, but it was an honour to the island fauna.

'We ought to take it alive!' Wilcox suggested.

'Rather!' exclaimed Service.

'That won't be easy,' said Cross.

'We'll try,' Briant decided.

The bird could not escape because its wings did not let it rise level with the ground, and its legs could not get a footing on the vertical walls. Wilcox had to slip down into the pit at the risk of receiving a few blows from the bird's beak, which might wound him severely. However, as he managed to throw his coat over the bird, to muffle its head, he escaped unharmed; and it was easy for him to bind its legs with two or three pocket handkerchiefs, tied to one another; and then, with a strong pull all together, the ostrich was hauled up to the bank.

'Now we've got it,' said Webb.

'And what shall we do with it?' asked Cross.

'That's simple enough,' said Service, who was never at a loss. 'We'll take it to the cave and tame it and we'll use it to ride upon. I'll look after it like my friend Jack in *The Swiss Family Robinson.*'

That it could be used in this fashion was doubtful, notwithstanding the precedent cited by Service; but as there was no difficulty in taking it to the cave, this was done.

When Gordon saw the nandu arrive he was a little alarmed at having another mouth to feed, but, remembering that the bird was a vegetarian, he gave it a cordial welcome. As to the youngsters, they were delighted to be near the bird—not too near, however—after it had been tied up with a long line. And when they heard that Service intended to train it for riding, they made him promise to give them a mount.

'Yes, if you're very good, babies,' replied Service, whom the youngsters already looked upon as a hero.

'We're sure to be that,' said Costar.

'What you, Costar?' Service asked him, 'you daring to ride this terrible animal?'

'Behind you—and holding on to you. Yes!'

'Do you remember how you felt when you were on the back of the turtle?'

'That isn't the same thing,' Costar protested. 'This thing doesn't go into the water.'

'But it goes into the air!' said Dole.

And the two little fellows walked off to think about this.

As may be imagined, as soon as they had got things into order at the cave, Gordon and his comrades had organised the regular daily life, giving everyone something to do, and taking particular care that the younger ones were not left to themselves. They, of course, asked for nothing better than to be set to work as far as their strength permitted, but why shouldn't they continue the lessons they had begun at Charman's school?

'We've got the books to help us go on with the work,' said Gordon. 'And what we've learnt we can teach, and it is only right we should give our young friends the benefit of it.'

'Yes,' answered Briant, 'and if we leave the island and get back to our friends, we can show them that we haven't wasted any time.'

It was agreed that a scheme of work should be drawn up, and after it had been submitted for general approval that it should be scrupulously adhered to. During the winter there would be many days when some of the boys would not be able to go out, and it was desirable for them to be profitably employed. The smallness of the cave was a great inconvenience, but it was decided to set to work forthwith to increase its size.

CHAPTER XII

THE COLONY

THE BOYS had often looked along the cliffs in the hope of finding another cave. If they had discovered one, they would have used it as a general store for what had now to be left out in the open. But the search had been in vain, and they had had to return to the scheme of enlarging their dwelling-place by digging into the walls.

There was no difficulty in doing this in the soft limestone, and the work would give them something to do during the winter, and could be finished by the return of the fine season if no collapse or infiltration occurred—as was not unlikely.

There was no need to take to blasting. The tools they had were sufficient for them to cut the hole for the chimney of the stove to be run out of, and Baxter had already been able, with some difficulty it is true, to enlarge the opening into the cave, so as to fit it with one of the doors from the schooner; and right and left of the door two embrasures had been cut in the wall, admitting light and air to the interior.

The bad weather had set in a week ago. Violent storms had swept across the island, but the cave did not have to face them, as it lay north and south. The rain and snow passed away over the crest of the cliff. The sportsmen had to leave the game along the vicinity of the lake, and the wild ducks, snipe, lapwing, rail, coot, and white pigeon, remained undisturbed. The lake and the river had not yet been frozen, but it only required a quiet night when the first dry cold would follow the storm for them to be covered with ice.

The work of enlarging the cave could thus be conveniently begun, and a start was made on 27th May.

The right wall was first attacked.

'If we dig on the slant,' said Briant, 'we may come out by the lakeside, and get a second entrance. That would give us a better lookout, and if the bad weather kept us in on one side, we might get out on the other.'

This would be an advantage, and there seemed no reason why the plan should not succeed.

Only forty or fifty feet separated the cave from the eastern face, and a gallery could easily be driven in the right direction, by compass, care being taken to avoid a roof-fall. Baxter's plan was to begin with a narrow tunnel, and then enlarge it till it was of the required size. The two rooms of the cave could then be united by a passage, which could be closed at both ends, and one or two galleries driven right and left of it to give additional room. The plan was evidently a good one, it allowed the rock to be dug out with due precaution, so that any sudden inrush of water could be satisfactorily dealt with, and the excavation abandoned if necessary.

For three days, from 27th to 30th May, the work went on favourably. The friable limestone could be cut with a knife; timbering had to be used to support the roof of the gallery, but that was easily managed. The spoil was taken outside, so as not to encumber the floor of the cave. There was not enough room for all to work at once, so the boys took it in turns. When the rain and snow ceased, Gordon and the elder boys took the raft to pieces, so that another use could be found for the deck and frame. And they overhauled the material stowed away against the cliff, which the tarpaulins did not cover satisfactorily.

The work of boring advanced gradually, not without many a stoppage to sound and make sure that progress was safe. Four or five feet had been excavated, when, on the afternoon of the 30th, something very unexpected happened.

Briant, on his knees in the hole, like a hewer in a coal-mine, thought he could hear a slight noise in the interior of the rock.

He stopped his picking and listened. Again the sound reached his ear.

To get out of the hole, and tell Gordon and Baxter, who were standing at the entrance, was the work of an instant.

'It's an illusion,' Gordon declared. 'You only imagined you heard it.'

'Take my place, then, put your ear to the wall and listen.'

Gordon got into the hole, and stayed there a few minutes.

'You're right,' he admitted, 'I can hear a sort of distant growling.'

Baxter went in, and confirmed this. 'What can it be?' he wondered.

'I can't think,' replied Gordon. 'We must tell Donagan and the others.'

'Not the youngsters,' said Briant, 'it would give them a scare.'

But as they all came in to dinner at the moment, the secret could not be kept.

Donagan, Wilcox, Webb, and Garnett, one after the other, went into the cavity and listened. But the sound must have ceased, for they heard nothing, and they concluded that their comrades had been mistaken.

Mistake or no mistake, it was resolved to continue the work, and as soon as the meal was over the digging recommenced. During the afternoon no noise was heard, but about nine in the evening the growling could be distinctly heard through the rock.

Fan ran into the hole and came out again at once with unmistakable signs of irritation, her coat bristling, her lips showing her teeth, and barking loudly, as if in reply to the growling in the rock.

And then the alarm mingled with surprise that the smaller boys had hitherto felt, gave place to fear. In vain Briant tried to soothe Dole, Costar, and even Jenkins and Iverson, but he at last got them to bed and to sleep.

Gordon and the others went on discussing this strange phenomenon. Every now and then the growling could be heard, and Fan would reply to it with a loud bark. Fatigue at last overcame them, and they went to bed, leaving Briant and Moko to watch; and till daylight profound silence reigned in French Den.

All were up early next morning. Baxter and Donagan crawled to the end of the hole. No sound could be heard. The dog ran to and fro without showing any uneasiness, and made no attempt to dash herself against the wall as she had done the night before.

'Let's get on with our work,' Briant suggested.

'Yes,' replied Baxter. 'There'll always be time to leave off if we hear any queer noise.'

'Isn't it possible,' said Donagan, 'that the growling was simply a spring in the rock?'

'Then we should hear it now,' said Wilcox, 'and we don't.'

'That is so,' agreed Gordon. 'I think it more likely to have come from the wind in some cranny leading down from the top of the cliff.'

'Let's go up on the top and see,' said Service.

The proposition was agreed to.

About fifty yards away there was a winding path, giving easy access to the summit of the hill. In a few minutes Baxter and two or three others were walking up it over French Den. Their journey was useless. The ridge was clothed with short close herbage, and no fissure was discoverable through which a current of air or a stream of water could find its way in. And when the boys got down again they knew no more about the strange phenomenon than the youngsters, who were explaining it to themselves as supernatural.

The digging was resumed and continued to the end of the day. There was no repetition of the noise, but Baxter examined the wall, and found that it sounded hollow. Was the tunnel going to end in a cave? Was it in this cave that the mysterious sound had arisen? There was nothing unlikely in the idea of a second excavation adjacent to the cavern in which they were working, and if such a thing existed, it would greatly reduce the labour. As may be imagined, the boys worked with extraordinary ardour, and the day was one of the most tiring they had yet experienced. Nevertheless it would have passed without incident had not Gordon noticed that the dog had disappeared.

Generally, at meal-times, Fan was to be found near her master's seat, but now her place was empty.

They called Fan. She did not answer. Gordon went to the door. He called her again. Complete silence.

Donagan and Wilcox went out, one along the bank of

the stream, the other along the shore of the lake—but they found no trace of the dog.

In vain was the search extended for a few hundred yards round French Den. Fan was not to be found.

Clearly the dog was not within call, for if she had been she would have answered. Had she strayed away? That was unlikely. Had she perished in the jaws of some wild beast? That was possible, and it was the best explanation of her disappearance that could be imagined.

It was nine at night. Thick darkness enveloped the cliff and the lake. The search had to be given up.

The boys went back to the cave. They were uneasy, and not only uneasy but grieved, to think that the dog had vanished, perhaps for ever.

Some of them stretched out on their beds, others sat round the table, not thinking of sleep. They seemed to be more alone than ever, more forsaken, removed farther from their country and friends.

Suddenly in the silence the noise broke out afresh. This time there was a long howl, and a cry of pain which lasted for nearly a minute.

'It's from over there, over there, that it comes!' exclaimed Briant, rushing to the tunnel.

They all rose as if waiting for an apparition. Terror had seized upon the little ones, who hid themselves under their bed-clothes.

When Briant came back he said—'There must be a cavern with its entrance at the foot of the cliff.'

'And some animals may take shelter during the night,' added Gordon.

'That's it,' Donagan agreed. 'And tomorrow we must try and find it.'

At this moment a bark was heard, and then a howl, coming from the interior of the rock.

'Can that be Fan,' asked Wilcox, 'fighting with some animal?'

Briant went back into the tunnel and listened with his ear against the wall. But there was nothing more. Whether Fan was there or not, clearly there must be a second excavation which ought to communicate with the exterior, probably by some gap in the brushwood thicket.

The night passed without either any more barking or howls being heard.

Next morning the search was begun at daybreak, but with no more result than the day before. Fan, though sought for and shouted for all over the neighbourhood, did not come back.

Briant and Baxter took turns at the digging, and pickaxe and shovel were kept constantly at work. During the morning the tunnel was made two feet longer. From time to time the boys stopped to listen, but they could hear nothing.

After dinner the digging began again. Precautions were taken in case a blow of the pickaxe were to knock through the wall and disclose some animal. The younger boys were taken out to the bank of the river. Gun in hand, Donagan, Wilcox, and Webb stood ready for anything that might happen.

About two Briant suddenly exclaimed. His pickaxe had gone through the limestone, which had collapsed leaving a good-sized hole.

He at once returned to his comrades, who did not know what to think—

But before they had time to open their mouths, an animal rushed down the tunnel and leapt into the cave.

It was Fan!

Yes, Fan, whose first action was to rush to a bowl of water and drink greedily. Then, she wagged her tail, without showing the least anger, and began to jump about in front of Gordon. Evidently there was no danger.

Briant then took a lantern and entered the tunnel, the others following him. Soon they were through the hole and in the middle of the gloomy excavation, to which no light penetrated from the outside.

It was a second cave, the same height and width as French Den but longer, and its floor was covered with fine sand for an area of about fifty square yards.

As the cavity seemed to have no communication with the exterior, it was feared that the air was not fit to breathe. But as the lamp in the lantern burned clearly, there must be some opening to admit the air. How else could Fan have got in?

Wilcox suddenly kicked his foot against something—feeling with his hand, he found it was cold and motionless.

Briant brought the light.

'It's the corpse of a jackal!' exclaimed Baxter.

'Yes! A jackal that our brave Fan has killed,' Briant agreed.

'And that explains our difficulty,' Gordon added.

But if a jackal or jackals had made this their haunt, how had they got in? The entrance could not be found.

Briant returned into French Den, and came out and ran along the cliff by the side of the lake. As he ran he shouted, and the boys in the cave replied. Soon he found a narrow entrance among the bushes, and level with the ground, through which the jackal had found a way in.

But since Fan had followed him a fall of earth had shut up the opening. This was soon found out, and thus everything was explained: the howling of the jackal and the barking of the dog, who for twenty-four hours had found it impossible to get out.

Great was the satisfaction at these things. Not only had Fan returned to her young masters, but labour was spared them. Here, 'ready-made,' as Dole said, was a large cave of which Baudoin had never suspected the existence. By making the opening larger, they would get a second door facing the lake that would be of great convenience to them. And naturally the boys, as they entered the new cave, gave three cheers, which Fan joined with a joyous bark.

Vigorously they set to work to make the tunnel practicable; this second excavation they called the 'hall', and its dimensions justified this. It would do for the dormitory and workroom, while the first cave would serve as kitchen and refectory; but Gordon proposed calling it the 'storeroom,' and his suggestion was adopted.

Soon they set to work to shift the beds and arrange them symmetrically on the sand of the hall, where there was plenty of room. Then the furniture of the schooner, the couches, armchairs, tables, cupboards and so forth, and—what was very important—the stoves from her saloons, were put in position. At the same time the entrance on the lake side was cleared out and enlarged so as to fit one of the schooner's doors—a job which cost Baxter a good deal of trouble. On each side of the door two new openings were made to give light until the evening, when a lamp hung from the centre of the roof illuminated the cave.

All this took a fortnight, and it was not finished any too

soon. The weather had begun to change. It was not as yet very cold; but the storms had become so violent that outdoor excursions were not to be thought of.

Such was the force of the wind that the waters of the lake were lashed into waves like a sea. The waves broke angrily on the beach, and a fishing-boat or native pirogue would have sought to cross it in vain. The yawl had to be dragged ashore to save its being washed away. At times the waters of the stream were held back by the wind, and overflowed the banks. Fortunately, neither the store-room nor the hall was directly exposed to the fury of the gale, which blew from the west; and the stoves and cooking-apparatus worked admirably, fed with dry wood, of which plenty had been gathered.

It was a great triumph to get everything from the schooner under cover, for the weather could not now damage the food. Gordon and his comrades, now imprisoned for the winter, had time to make themselves comfortable. They had enlarged the passage and dug out two deep side-chambers, one of which was closed with a door, and reserved for the ammunition, to avoid any danger of an explosion.

Although the gunners could not get away from French Den, yet there were enough aquatic birds close handy to fill Moko's larder, although he did not always manage to cook them so as to get rid of their marshy taste.

When things were in order Gordon proposed drawing up a programme to which all would have to submit when it had received general approval. How long were they to stay on this island? When they came to leave it, would it not be as well to think that the time had not been wasted? With the books from the schooner's library the bigger boys could increase their knowledge while they taught the younger ones. An excellent task, which would usefully and agreeably occupy the long hours of winter!

However, before the programme was finished, another measure was adopted.

On the night of June 10th, after supper they were in the hall, seated round the stove, when conversation turned on this chance of giving names to the chief geographical features of the island.

'That would be very useful,' said Briant.

'Yes, let's have names,' Iverson agreed, 'and let us have good ones.'

'Let's do what is done by the other Crusoes, real or imaginary,' Webb suggested.

'And really,' Gordon pointed out 'we're only—'

'A Crusoe school!' Service interrupted.

'Besides,' continued Gordon, 'with names for the bay, the stream, the forests, the lake, the cliff, the marshes and capes, we'll find it easier to identify them.'

The motion was adopted at once, and there was nothing left to do but to think of suitable names.

'We've got Schooner Bay, where the yacht was wrecked,' said Donagan, 'and I think we might as well keep to the name we're used to.'

'Right you are,' Cross assented.

'And in the same way we'll keep the name of French Den for our cave, in memory of poor Baudoin.'

There was no objection to this even from Donagan, though the suggestion was made by Briant.

'And now,' asked Wilcox, 'what shall we call the river which flows into Schooner Bay?'

'Zealand River,' said Baxter; 'it will remind us of our country.'

'Agreed! Agreed!'

Carried unanimously.

'And the lake?' asked Garnett.

'As you named the river Zealand in memory of your country,' said Donagan, 'you might as well call the lake Family Lake to remind you of your relatives.'

This was also agreed to without a dissentient; and similarly the name Auckland Hill was given to the cliff. The cape at the end, whence Briant thought he had seen the sea to the eastward was called, at his suggestion, False Sea Point.

The other names adopted were Trap Woods, for that part of the forest where the trap had been found; Bog Wood, for the part between Schooner Bay and the cliff; South Moor, for the marsh on the south of the island; Dike Creek, for the brook where they had found the causeway; Wreck Coast, for the coast where the yacht had come ashore; Games Terrace, for the tract between the banks of the river and lake where the games were to take place.

The other parts of the island were named as they were discovered, and the names referred to what had happened there at the time. It, however, seemed advisable to give names to the principal promontories marked on Baudoin's map, so that there was a North Cape, and a South Cape, and it was agreed to give the three western headlands the names of the nations represented in the colony: a British Cape, American Cape and French Cape.

We said colony! Yes! The word was proposed as a reminder that the occupation was no longer provisionary; and naturally it came from Gordon, who was more interested in organising ways to live in the new territory than to find a way out of it. The boys were no longer the castaways from the schooner; they were the colonists of an island.

But what island? The island itself wanted naming.

'Here! Here! I know what to call it!' Costar exclaimed.

'You know, do you?' Donagan asked.

'You're getting on, young Costar!' said Garnett.

'Of course you'll call it Baby Island?' Service grinned.

'Come, don't chaff him,' said Briant, 'let's hear what he's got to say.'

The little fellow did not speak.

'Speak up, Costar,' Briant urged him. 'I'm sure your idea is a good one. What is it?'

'Well,' Costar suggested, 'as we all come from Charman's school we ought to call it Charman Island!'

They could not do better than this, and the name was received with general applause—which made Costar look quite important.

Charman Island! Really the name had the true geographical ring about it, and would not disgrace any atlas!

The ceremony being at an end to the general satisfaction, the time had come to go to bed, when Briant begged to be allowed to speak.

'My friends,' he said, 'now that we've named our island, wouldn't it be better to elect a leader to govern it?'

'A leader!' asked Donagan.

'Yes. It seems to me that things would go better,' continued Briant, 'if one of us had some authority over the others! What's done in every other country oughtn't we to do in Charman Island?'

'Yes! A leader! Let's have a leader!'

'Let's have a leader,' said Donagan, 'but on condition that it's only for some stated time—a year, for example.'

'But he can be re-elected,' added Briant.

'Agreed! Who's it to be?' asked Donagan anxiously.

The jealous lad seemed to have only one fear, that in spite of all he could say the choice would fall on Briant. He was quickly undeceived.

'Who is it to be?' replied Briant. 'Why, the wisest of us, to be sure, our friend Gordon!'

'Yes! Yes! Three cheers for Gordon!'

Gordon would at first have refused the honour they wanted to bestow on him, saying that he was better fitted to organise than to command. But he foresaw the trouble that the passions of these young people, now almost as ardent as if they had been men, might lead to in the future, and he felt that his authority might not be without its value.

And in this way Gordon was proclaimed Governor of the little colony of Charman Island.

CHAPTER XIII

WINTER QUARTERS

THE WINTER season had definitely set in on Charman Island by the beginning of May. How long would it last? Five months or less if the latitude were the same as that of New Zealand. So Gordon prepared for the rigours of a long winter.

The young American made careful notes of his meteorological observations. He found that as the winter did not begin until May—that is, two months before July—which answers to January in the northern hemisphere, it would probably last for two months afterwards, or until about the middle of September, when the storms prevalent about the time of the equinox would prolong it. So the young colonists might be kept at French Den till the early days of October before they could make a long excursion either across or round Charman Island. He had thus to draw up a programme of such daily work as would be the best for the life in the cave.

And in the first place he decided to have nothing to do with the fag system they had been used to at Charman's School. His whole effort was directed to accustoming the boys to the idea that they were almost men, and had to act as such. There were to be no fags at French Den: the younger boys were not to be the servants of the elders.

Their library contained a few books of science and travel, so that the bigger boys could pursue their studies only to a limited extent. But the difficulties of existence, the constant struggle to supply their wants, the need for exercising the judgment of imagination in the presence of eventualities of all sorts, would teach them to regard life seriously. As it was natural that they should be the educators of their young companions, it would be their duty to teach them.

In order not to overburden the youngsters with work too great for their age, every opportunity would be taken of exercising their bodies as well as their minds. When the weather permitted they would be allowed out, in suitable clothes of course, to run and enjoy themselves in the fresh air, or work at such manual labour as their strength allowed. In short, the scheme was drawn up on the four main principles which form the basis of English education:—

'If you're frightened at anything, do it.'
'Never lose a chance of doing your very best.'
'Never fear fatigue, for nothing you can do is useless.'
'A healthy body means a healthy mind.'

This was agreed at a general meeting of the boys.

For two hours every morning, and two hours every evening they would all work in the hall. Taking it in turns, Briant, Donagan, Cross and Baxter of the fifth form, and Wilcox and Webb of the fourth, would hold classes for their schoolfellows of the third, second, and first forms. They would teach them mathematics, geography, history, supplementing the knowledge they had acquired at school from the books in the library. This would prevent their forgetting what they already knew. Twice a week, on Sunday and Thursday, there would be a debate on some subject of science, or history, or some actual happening, and in this all would take part.

Gordon, as leader of the colony, would see that the

programme was carried out without modification, unless something occurred that rendered it impossible.

To begin with, arrangements were made regarding the duration of time. They had the yacht's almanac, but each day had to be regularly marked off, and they had watches, but these had to be regularly wound up and adjusted to keep exact time. Two of the bigger boys were entrusted with this duty: Wilcox had charge of the watches, Baxter of the almanac. And to Webb fell the duty of recording the daily readings of the barometer and thermometer.

The next thing was to start a log of all that happened during their stay on Charman Island. Baxter volunteered for this, and thanks to him the *French Den Journal* was written up with minute exactitude.

A work of no less importance, and which could be no longer delayed, was washing the linen; there was no lack of soap, and this was lucky considering the mess the youngsters got into when they played on the terrace or fished in the stream. In vain Gordon cautioned them, and grumbled at them, and threatened to punish them; dirty they would get in spite of all he could do. There was no doubt as to who should do the washing: Moko knew all about it; but as he could not manage it all, the bigger boys had to assist him.

The day after this programme had been agreed upon was Sunday, and the way in which that day is kept in England and America is well known. In the morning the young colonists went for a walk along the banks of Family Lake. But as it was extremely cold the boys, after an outing of a couple of hours, were glad to get back to their warm hall and a hot dinner in the store-room, carefully prepared by the clever master-cook of French Den. In the evening there was a concert, in which Garnett's accordion took the place of an orchestra, and the singing, more or less out of tune, was of the true Anglo-Saxon type. The only boy with a really musical voice was Jack, but in his present inexplicable humour he would take no part in his companions' occupations, and refused to sing when they asked him.

The day, which had begun with a short address by 'the Reverend Gordon,' as Service called him, ended with a few minutes' prayer in the hall: and by ten o'clock all the boys were asleep under the protection of Fan, whom they could trust in the event of anything suspicious.

Dpring June the cold gradually increased. Webb reported that the barometer was steady at just above twenty-seven inches, and the thermometer was from eighteen to twenty degrees below freezing. As soon as the wind, which blew from the south, shifted towards the west the temperature rose a little, and the surroundings of French Den were covered with a deep snowfall. The snow was not unwelcome, as it afforded an opportunity for a grand snowballing match, in which a few of the boys suffered severely, notably Jack, who stood looking on. A ball thrown furiously by Cross missed its mark and hit him hard enough to make him cry.

'I didn't do it on purpose,' Cross protested with the usual excuse of the clumsy.

'Perhaps not,' Briant had noticed his brother's eye, 'but you shouldn't throw so hard.'

'Well, why did he get in the way?' Cross wanted to know. 'Why isn't he playing?'

'What a fuss about a little bruise!' Donagan exclaimed.

'Perhaps it isn't very serious,' answered Briant, seeing that Donagan wished to interfere, 'but I'll ask Cross not to do it again.'

'How can he manage that,' asked Donagan jeeringly, 'if he didn't do it on purpose?'

'I don't know what business it is of yours, Donagan,' said Briant; 'it only concerns Cross and me—'

'And it concerns me too, Briant, if that's how you take it?' Donagan replied.

'As you please—and when you please,' Briant crossed his arms defiantly.

'Let's have it now, then,' put in Donagan.

At this moment Gordon came up, just in time to prevent the quarrel from ending in a fight.

He decided that Donagan was in the wrong. And Donagan had to submit, and much to his disgust went back to French Den. But it was to be feared that some other incident would soon bring the rivals to blows.

The snow went on falling for two days. To amuse their young comrades, Service and Garnett made a big snowman, with a big head and an enormous nose. And it may as well be confessed that although during the day Dole and Costar were brave enough to pelt the figure with snowballs, yet at night, when the darkness had made it seem larger, they could not look at it without being frightened.

'Oh! the cowards!' Iverson and Jenkins pretended to be very brave, although they were no less terrified than their young companions.

At the end of June their amusements had to be given up. The snow, piled up to three or four feet thick, made it almost impossible to get out. To venture more than a few hundred yards from French Den was to risk being unable to return.

The young colonists were thus kept in for a fortnight, until 9th July. The work did not suffer; on the contrary, the daily programme was strictly adhered to. The discussions took place on the proper days, and in this they took delight, and it is not surprising that Donagan, with his facility of speech and advanced education, held the first place. But why was he so proud? His vanity spoilt all his brilliant qualities.

Although the hours of recreation had to be passed in the hall, the general health did not suffer, thanks to the ventilation obtained through the passage. The question of hygiene was important. If one of the boys was to fall ill how could they give him the needful attention? Fortunately they escaped with a few colds and sore throats, which rest and warm drinks soon got rid of.

There was another question to be solved. So far the water had been got from the stream at low tide when the brackishness had disappeared. But when the surface of the stream was frozen over this would no longer be possible. Gordon consulted with Baxter, his 'civil engineer,' as to what was best to be done. Baxter, after consideration, proposed to run a conduit a few feet below the bank so that the water it contained would not freeze on its way to the store-room. This would have been a difficult job if Baxter had not had at his disposal the lead pipes from the yacht's lavatory, and so, after many attempts, the water was at last laid on into the interior of the store-room. For lighting there was still enough oil for the lanterns, but after the winter, they would have to make candles out of the fat, which Moko had carefully preserved.

The feeding of the little colony also gave much trouble, for neither the huntsmen nor the fishermen could furnish their usual tribute. A few animals, driven by hunger, came prowling about Game Terrace; but these were jackals that Donagan and Cross scared away by firing a

WINTER QUARTERS

gun. One day they came in a troop—there were about twenty of them—and the doors of the hall and store-room had to be barricaded against them. An invasion of carnivores made fierce by hunger would have been formidable. But Fan gave the alarm in time, and they did not force their way into French Den.

Under these unfortunate conditions Moko was obliged to make inroads upon the provisions from the yacht, which it had been agreed to make last as long as possible. Gordon never willingly gave permission for them to be used, and it was with distress he saw his column of expenses lengthening while that of his receipts remained stationary. However, as there was a large stock of ducks and bustards which had been hermetically sealed in casks after being half cooked, Moko was able to use them as well as a certain quantity of salmon preserved in brine. But it should not be forgotten that French Den had fifteen mouths to satisfy, and these with appetites of from eight to fourteen years old.

But during this winter, there was not a complete lack of fresh meat. Wilcox, who was quite an expert in trapping, kept several 'figure 4' traps laid on the river-bank with success, and aided by his companions he rigged up a few vertical nets supported by long sticks; the birds flying across the stream from South Moor were often caught in the mesh, and although most of them got away, yet occasionally enough were taken to form a welcome addition to the day's meals.

But it was the nandu which gave the most trouble; and it must be confessed that the taming of this wild animal made no progress, although Service was specially charged with his education.

'What a racer it will be!' he would repeat, although he did not yet see how he could ride it.

As the nandu did not eat flesh, Service had to go out and search for its daily provision of herbs and roots under two or three feet of snow. But what would he not have done for the nourishment of his pet?

If it got rather thin during this interminable winter, this was not the fault of its faithful guardian, and there was reason to hope that when the spring came it would recover its normal plumpness.

On 9th July, when Briant went out first thing in the morning, he found that the wind had suddenly gone back to the south.

The cold had become so keen that Briant at once went into the hall, and notified Gordon of the change of temperature.

'That's what I feared,' Gordon replied, 'and I shan't be surprised if we have to put up with several months of very severe winter.'

'That would show,' Briant commented, 'that the yacht drifted much farther south than we supposed.'

'I daresay,' replied Gordon; 'but our atlas doesn't show any island like this on the boundary of the Antarctic Ocean!'

'It's inexplicable, and really I don't know where we shall go if we manage to leave Charman Island.'

'Leave our island!' insisted Gordon. 'Are you always thinking of that?'

'Always!' said Briant, 'If we could build a seaworthy boat, I shouldn't hesitate to go on a voyage of discovery.'

'All right!' Gordon agreed, 'But there's no hurry. Wait a little till we've got our colony into order.'

'Eh?' said Briant. 'You forget we have left our fathers and mothers.'

'Of course—of course,' Gordon admitted. 'But we're not so badly off here! We're getting on, and I'm beginning to ask myself what it is we haven't got.'

'Many things, Gordon,' Briant did not care to prolong the conversation on this subject. 'For instance we're running short of fuel.'

'Oh! All the forests in the island aren't burnt yet.'

'No. But we ought to replenish our stock of wood, for it's nearly at an end.'

'We'll see about that today. What does the thermometer say?'

The thermometer in the store-room showed only 41°, although the stove was doing its best. But when the instrument was taken outside, and exposed against the outer wall, it went down to zero.

This cold was intense, and it would certainly increase if the weather stayed clear and dry for a few weeks. Already, notwithstanding the roaring of the stoves in the hall and the cooking-range, the temperature was perceptibly falling inside French Den.

About nine, after breakfast, it was decided to go to Trap Woods, and bring in a stock of fuel.

When the atmosphere is calm the lowest temperatures can be supported with impunity: it is during the bitter wind that hands and face are frost-bitten, and life is in danger. Fortunately on this day the wind was extremely feeble, and the sky without a cloud, as if the air were frozen. In place of the soft snow into which, on the night before, the legs would have sunk, the surface was now as hard as iron, and to avoid falling the boys had to walk as carefully as if they were on Family Lake or Zealand

River, which were now entirely frozen over. With a few pairs of snow-shoes, such as are used by the natives of polar regions, or even with a sledge drawn by dogs or reindeer, the lake could have been explored from north to south in a few hours.

But no such expedition was intended today. To go to the neighbouring forest to replenish the stock of fuel, that was the immediate necessity; and to bring enough to the cave would be arduous work, if it had to be transported in the arms or on the back. But Moko had an idea. The big table in the store-room, strongly built, and measuring twelve feet by four, wouldn't that do for a sledge if the legs were turned uppermost? Why, certainly, and with four of the bigger boys dragging it by cords attached to its legs, they set off to Trap Woods.

The younger ones, with red noses and healthy cheeks, frisked along in front, and Fan set them the example. Occasionally they caught hold of the table, not without disputes and running fights, but all in fun, and at the risk only of a fall, which could do them no harm. Their shouts resounded with extraordinary clearness in the cold, dry atmosphere. And, indeed, it was quite refreshing to see all the little colony in good humour and good health.

Everything was white as far as the eye could see between Auckland Hill and Family Lake. The trees, with their rimy branches loaded with glittering crystals, rose near and far in masses, as in a fairy garden. Over the surface of the lake the birds flew in flocks. Donagan and Cross had not forgotten to bring their guns—a wise precaution, for footprints were noticed that must have been made by wild animals other than jackals, cougars, and jaguars.

'Perhaps they are the wild cats they call "pajeros,"' Gordon suggested.

'Oh!' Costar shrugged his shoulders, 'if they're only cats—'

'And tigers are only cats,' Jenkins pointed out.

'Is it true, Service,' asked Costar, 'that these cats are dangerous?'

'Quits true,' said Service. 'And they scrag little boys as easily as they do mice.'

This answer made Costar rather uneasy.

The half-mile between French Den and Trap Woods was soon covered, and the young wood-cutters got to work. The axe was laid only to such trees as were sizeable: these were stripped of their smaller branches so as to yield not only faggots which would blaze away in a moment, but good-sized blocks that would come in useful for the stoves and range. Then the table-sledge was heavily loaded, but it slipped along so easily that before noon it had made two journeys.

After a meal the work went on till four, when the day began to close in. It was tiring, and as there was no need to carry anything to excess Gordon called the boys off, intending to return in the morning. And when Gordon ordered they had to obey.

Besides, as soon as they returned to French Den, they could saw the blocks up, split them, and stow them away, and that would occupy them till it was time to go to bed.

For six days this woodcutting went on without a break, and enough fuel was collected to last for many weeks. Of course all this wood could not be stowed in the storeroom; but there was no reason why most of it should not remain in safety against the cliff near the door.

The 15th July, according to the almanac, was St.

Swithin's Day, which in England corresponds to St. Medard's Day in France.

'Then,' said Briant, 'as its raining today, are we going to have forty days' rain?'

'Well,' said Service, 'I don't see how that can matter, as we're in the winter. If it had been summer—'

And, in fact, the inhabitants of the southern hemisphere have no occasion to bother themselves with the sinister influences of either of the wet saints, who are winter saints in the antipodes.

But the rain did not continue, the wind returned to the south-east, and it became so cold that Gordon would not allow any of the youngsters to set foot out of doors.

In the first week in August the thermometer sank to 14° below zero, and the breath of those who for a moment exposed themselves to the air condensed into snow. The hand could not touch a piece of metal without a sharp pain like burning. The most careful precautions had to be taken to keep the indoors temperature sufficiently high.

A most painful fortnight followed. All suffered, more or less, from the want of exercise. Briant could not see without feeling anxious the pale looks of the youngsters, whose colour had disappeared. However, thanks to the hot drinks, which were always obtainable, with the exception of a few colds and bronchial troubles, the young people escaped without much damage.

On August 16th, the air underwent a change, as the wind shifted into the west, and the thermometer rose to 10°, a temperature that was supportable if the atmosphere was calm.

Donagan, Briant, Service, Wilcox and Baxter decided to visit Schooner Bay. By starting early they could get back before night.

WINTER QUARTERS

They wanted to find out if the coast were visited by any number of those amphibians of which they had seen a few at the time of the wreck; and they would also replace the flag, of which only a few rags could remain after the storms of winter. And, at Briant's suggestion, they could fix to the signal-mast a map indicating the position of French Den, in case anybody landed on the coast after seeing the flag.

Gordon agreed to the expedition, although he laid stress on the need for getting back before night, and the boys started early on the 19th, before it was daylight. The sky was clear, and the moon lit up the landscape with the pale rays of its last quarter. Six miles to the bay was not much of a distance for the well-rested legs.

The distance was soon covered. The swamp of Bog Wood being frozen over, there was no need to go round it, and by nine Donagan and his comrades had reached the beach.

'There's a flock of birds,' Wilcox pointed to the reef, where thousands of birds, like large ducks, with their beaks elongated like a mussel-shell, were giving vent to a cry as piercing as it was disagreeable.

'You would say they were little soldiers, whose general was reviewing them,' said Service.

'They're only penguins,' answered Baxter, 'and they aren't worth a shot.'

These stupid birds, holding themselves almost upright because their feet were set so far back, did not try to move and could have been knocked down with a stick. Donagan might, perhaps, have indulged in useless carnage; but Briant having had the wisdom to say nothing, the penguins were left alone.

But if the birds were of no use, there were other animals whose fat would do for lighting French Den during the next winter. These were the seals, of the horn-seal species, who were taking their ease on the reef, then covered with a thick bed of ice. But to kill them the boys would have to cut off their retreat, for when Briant and his comrades approached they took flight with many extraordinary antics, and disappeared into the sea. Evidently an expedition to capture these animals would have to be organised later on.

After having lunched on the few provisions they had brought, the boys set to work to examine the whole stretch of the bay.

One long white sheet extended from Zealand River to False Point. Except for the penguins and sea-birds, the petrels and gulls, the birds seemed to have forsaken the beach for the interior in search of food.

Two or three feet of snow lay on the beach, and all that remained of the schooner had been hidden by it. The lines of seaweed on the near side of the breakers showed that Schooner Bay had not been invaded by the high tides of the equinox.

The sea was still deserted, as far as could be seen, right up to the horizon that Briant had not looked upon for three long months. And beyond, hundreds of miles away, was New Zealand that he did not despair of seeing again.

Baxter busied himself in hoisting the new flag which he had brought with him, and nailing to the flagstaff the map giving the position of French Den, six miles up stream. Then, about one in the afternoon, they started homewards.

On the way Donagan shot a brace of pintail and lapwing which were skimming over the river; and towards four, as dusk was coming on, they reached the cave. Gor-

WINTER QUARTERS

don was told of all that had happened, and agreed that the seals should be attacked as soon as the weather permitted.

The winter was in fact nearly over. During the last week of August and the first week of September, the seabreeze regained its supremacy. A series of squalls brought on a great increase of temperature. The snow began to melt, the surface of the lake to break up with a deafening noise. The bergs that did not melt in the lake were swept into the river, and, piled one on the other, formed a barrier that did not clear away till 19th September.

And at last the winter had passed. Owing to the precautions they had taken, the little colony had not suffered excessively. All had kept in good health, and the studies having been attended to zealously, Gordon had hardly had one complaint to deal with.

One day, however, he had had to chastise Dole, whose conduct required an exemplary punishment.

Several times the obstinate boy had refused to do what he was told, and Gordon had reprimanded him, but he took no notice. And in the end Gordon sentenced him to be whipped.

And so Dole received a birching at the hands of Wilcox, who had been selected by lot for the post of public executioner. And the example had its effect in preventing any recurrence of insubordination.

On September 10th six months had elapsed since the schooner had been lost on the reefs of Charman Island.

CHAPTER XIV

A JOURNEY NORTHWARDS

WITH THE fine weather now in prospect the young colonists intended to carry out several of the schemes they had thought about during the long winter.

To the west it was only too obvious that there was no land near the island. Was it the same in the north and south? Did the island belong to any archipelago or group in the Pacific? According to Baudoin's map it certainly did not. Nevertheless there might be islands in these parts, for Baudoin had had no telescope or field-glasses, and Auckland Hill was only high enough to command a horizon of a few miles. The boys with their instruments might discover what had been beyond the powers of the survivor of the *Duguay Trouin*.

According to the map, Charman Island measured no more than twelve miles across to the eastward of French Den. In a line with Schooner Bay the coast was deeply indented, and an exploring party might profitably be despatched that way.

But before going farther afield the district around Auckland Hill, Family Lake, and Trap Woods ought to be explored. What were its resources? Was it rich in useful trees or shrubs? To ascertain this an expedition was decided upon, to start early in November.

But although in an astronomical sense spring had commenced, yet the island was in so high a latitude that its influence had not made itself apparent. The month of

September and the first half of October were distinguished by a spell of bad weather; and there were still sharp frosts, which did not last, the winds being so variable. During this equinoctial period the atmospheric troubles were very violent, as had been those which had brought the schooner across the Pacific. The heavy squalls seemed to shake the hill, and when they swept from over the South Moor, where there was no obstacle to check them, bitter was the blast they brought from the Antarctic Ocean. Twenty times the wind blew in the store-room door and penetrated down the passage to the hall; and this made things worse than they had been in the winter, when the thermometer went down below zero. And it was not only the wind, but the rain and the hail, which the lads had to contend with.

To make things worse, the birds seemed to have disappeared as if they had sought refuge in parts of the island less exposed to the equinoctial gales, and the fish had also gone, probably frightened away by the disturbance of the waters, which roared along the shore of the lake.

The boys in French Den were not idle. The snow had gone, so that the table could no longer be used as a vehicle, so Baxter set about making a cart, on which heavy weights could be moved.

His idea was to use two of the wheels of the schooner's windlass; but he did not succeed without a number of trials which a skilled artisan would have avoided. The wheels were toothed, and after trying in vain to break the teeth, Baxter had to fill up the intervals with wedges of wood and fasten them round with an iron hoop. Then the two wheels were fixed to an iron bar, and on this axle-tree a platform of planks was laid. It was a very rudimentary vehicle, but such as it was it would come in very useful. But as there were neither horses, mules, nor donkeys in the island, the boys would have to drag it themselves.

If they could only have come across a few trained quadrupeds what trouble they would have been spared! Why was the fauna of Charman Island so much richer in birds than in animals? With the example of Service's ostrich, would they ever be able to train the birds to work for them?

The nandu had lost nothing of its wildness. It would let no one approach it without defending itself with its beak and claws; it tried its utmost to break the cord which held it, and if it had done so it would soon have been lost under the trees in Trap Wood.

But Service was not discouraged. He had naturally given the nandu the name of 'Hurricane,' like Master Jack's ostrich in *The Swiss Family Robinson*. But although he did his best to tame the restive creature, neither gentleness nor severity had any effect.

'And yet,' said he one day, referring to the romance of De Wyss, which he was for ever reading. 'Jack managed to tame his ostrich in a very short time.'

'Probably he did,' Gordon replied. 'But between your hero and yourself, Service, there's exactly the same difference as between his ostrich and yours.'

'And what's that?'

'Simply the difference between imagination and reality.'

'What does that matter?' protested Service. 'I'll get the better of this ostrich, or it shall tell me why.'

'Very good!' Gordon laughed. 'I'll be as much surprised to hear it tell you as to see it obey you.'

In spite of the jokes of his schoolmates, Service had

decided to mount his nandu as soon as weather permitted. In imitation of his hero he had made a sort of harness out of sailcloth and a cap with blinkers. Had not Jack guided his bird by dropping a blinker over the right or left eye, as the case might be? And why then should not his imitator succeed as he had succeeded? Service had even made a plaited collar to fix on the neck of the animal, which would willingly have dispensed with the ornament. But as to the cap, it was almost impossible to get it on to its head.

The equinox was nearly over. The sun was gaining in power, and the sky was clearing. It was mid-October. The sun lent its warmth to the shrubs and trees, which were again beginning to become green.

The boys could now be out of doors all day. The warm clothes, thick cloth trousers, and oilskins were beaten, repaired, folded, and carefully put away after being ticketed by Gordon. The young colonists, more at ease in their lighter garments, greeted the return of summer with gladness, and one hope never left them, that of making some discoveries that would improve their position. During the summer might not a ship visit these parts? And if she passed in sight of Charman Island, why shouldn't she send men ashore when she noticed the flag on the crest of Auckland Hill?

During the second fortnight in October, many excursions were made within a radius of two miles round French Den. The hunters went out, and the bill of fare soon felt the effects, although powder and shot were severely economised. Wilcox went forth with his nets and snares, and caught several brace of tinamous and bustards, and even a few small hares. Several times a day he had to visit his nets, for the jackals and paperos were quite equal to being beforehand with him, and helping themselves to what he had caught.

Donagan killed a few peccaries and guaculis—pigs and deer of small stature—which have savoury flesh; but nobody regretted he could not get near the nandus, as Service's success with Hurricane was not encouraging. This was clearly shown on the morning of the 26th, when the obstinate boy tried to mount his ostrich, on which it was not without difficulty he had got the harness.

The boys were all out on the terrace to witness the interesting experiment, the younger ones regarding their schoolfellow with a feeling of envy mingled with anxiety. At the decisive moment they hesitated to ask Service to give them a ride. The bigger boys shook their heads, and Gordon tried to dissuade Service from attempting what seemed so dangerous. But it was to no purpose, and they let him have his own way.

Garnett and Baxter held the bird, which had its eyes covered with the blinkers from the cap, and Service, after many attempts, succeeded in getting on its back. Then in a somewhat hesitating voice, he said, 'Let go!'

The nandu, deprived of the use of its eyes, remained motionless with the boy clinging firmly to it with his legs. But as soon as the blinkers were lifted by the cord that served for reins, the bird gave a tremendous leap, and shot off in the direction of the forest.

Service was helpless to guide his steed, which fled with the speed of an arrow. In vain he tried to stop it by dropping the blinkers; with a knock of its head it shook off the cap, and this slipped down its neck, to which Service was clinging with both arms. Then a violent shock unseated the cavalier, and he fell to the ground just as his mount was about to disappear under the trees of Trap Woods.

Service's comrades ran up, and when they arrived the ostrich was out of sight.

Fortunately Service had rolled on to the grass and sustained no injury.

'The crazy brute!' he exclaimed. 'Ah! If I catch you—'

'But you'll never catch him,' Donagan told him.

'Well,' Webb pointed out, 'your friend Jack is a better horseman than you are.'

'My nandu wasn't tame enough,' said Service.

'And never would be,' said Gordon. 'Console yourself with thinking that you should never have had anything to do with the creature, and don't forget that in De Wyss' romance you mustn't believe all you read.'

So the adventure ended, and the youngsters had no reason to regret that they had not had their ostrich-ride.

In the first week of November the weather appeared favourable for an expedition of some duration to the western shore of Family Lake and thence to the northward. The sky was clear, the heat supportable, and there would be nothing imprudent in passing a few nights in the open air.

Naturally the hunters formed part of the expedition, and this time Gordon thought it best to go with them. Those who remained at French Den were left in charge of Briant and Garnett. Later on Briant, it was arranged, would lead another expedition to the lower part of the lake, coasting its shores in the boat and perhaps crossing it.

Everything being arranged, Gordon, Donagan, Baxter,

A JOURNEY NORTHWARDS

Wilcox, Webb, Cross, and Service started on 5th November.

At French Den no change was made in the usual daily round. In the hours not consecrated to work, Iverson, Jenkins, Dole, and Costar spent their time in fishing in the river, which was their favourite recreation. Moko stayed at home; but do not think that the explorers suffered from the want of a cook. Wasn't Service with them? Wasn't he cook's mate? And hadn't he given his skill as a reason for accompanying the expedition, in which he might perhaps recover his ostrich?

Gordon, Donagan, and Wilcox each carried a gun and a revolver. Hunting-knives and two axes completed their equipment. Powder and shot were not to be used except in self-defence, or to bring down something to eat if they failed to obtain provisions in a more economical way. To this end Baxter brought his lasso and the bolas, in whose use practice had made him expert. A very quiet boy, but a clever one, he had quickly made himself master of these weapons against targets that could not move, but whether he would succeed with animals at full speed remained to be seen.

Gordon had brought with him the Halkett india-rubber boat: shut up in its bag it was very portable and weighed only a few pounds, and the map showed two tributaries of the lake where it might be useful if there were no ford.

According to the map, of which Gordon carried a copy, the western shore of Family Lake was about eighteen miles long, reckoning the ins and outs. The exploration would take a full three days going and returning, if no delays were met with.

Gordon and his companions, preceded by Fan, left Trap Woods to the left, and walked at a good pace along the sandy shore. When they had gone more than two miles they were farther away than any of the excursions had gone since quarters had been taken up at the cave. Hereabouts a few cortadera bushes grew in clumps, among which the tallest of the party disappeared. This hindered their progress, but this was not to be regretted, as Fan stopped and pointed before one of a group of half a dozen holes in the ground.

Evidently she had scented some animal. Donagan was bringing his gun to his shoulder when Gordon stopped him.

'Spare your powder, Donagan,' he told him.

'Perhaps our breakfast may be there?' the young hunter protested.

'And our dinner too?' Service added kneeling beside the hole.

'If they are, we can get them out without wasting any lead,' Wilcox pointed out.

'And how?' asked Webb.

'By smoking them out.'

Between the clumps of cortadera the ground was covered with dry twigs, and Wilcox soon lit a bundle of them in front of one of the holes. A minute later appeared a dozen half-suffocated rodents trying in vain to escape. They were tucutuco hares, and Service and Webb soon despatched a few with the axes, while Fan strangled three others with her teeth.

'They'll make an excellent meal!' said Gordon.

'And I'll see after them,' Service was eager to begin his duties as master cook. 'I'll start on them at once if you like.'

'At our first halt,' Gordon agreed.

It took half an hour to get through this miniature forest

of cortadera bushes. Beyond appeared the beach with a long line of dunes, its sand so fine and light as to blow up with the least breeze.

The flank of Auckland Hill was now more than two miles away to the westward because of the direction of the cliff. All this part of the island was covered with the dense forest which Briant and his companions had crossed in their first expedition, and through which ran the stream they had called Dike Creek.

According to the map, this stream flowed into the lake; and it was at its mouth that the boys arrived at about eleven, having covered six miles since their departure. Here they halted at the foot of a superb parasol pine. A fire of wood was lighted between two large stones, and in a few minutes two of the tucutucos, skinned and drawn by Service, were roasting before a crackling fire. And while Fan lay and sniffed the grateful perfume of the venison, the cook took care to turn the spit so that the meat should not spoil.

There was not much fault to be found with Service's first attempt. There was enough to eat, and the meat was savoury with the flavour of the aromatic herbs on which the rodents feed; except for a few biscuits in place of bread, the provisions brought in the bags were left untouched.

The meal over, a start was made across the creek, and as there was a ford, there was no need to waste time getting out the boat.

The shore of the lake, now becoming marshy, forced them to keep away to the edge of the forest. The species of trees did not change—magnificently grown beeches, birches, green oaks, and pines of different kinds fringed the way. Numbers of charming birds leapt from branch to branch, black woodpeckers with red crests, flycatchers with white tufts, wrens, with finches, larks, and thrushes singing or whistling in full power. Afar in the sky hovered condors, ururbus, and a few pairs of caracaras, the voracious eagle of South America.

Probably in remembrance of Robinson Crusoe, Service regretted that the parrot family was not represented in the island's ornithology. If he could not tame an ostrich, he might succeed with one of those talkative birds; but not one did he see.

In short, there was abundance of birds and animals for food; and Gordon could not refuse Donagan the pleasure of shooting a moderate-sized peccary, which would do for breakfast in the morning, if not for dinner that night.

There was no need to enter the forest, and progress was comparatively easy. And they continued skirting the trees until five, when the second watercourse, which was about forty feet wide, barred the way. This was one of the outlets of the lake, and flowed round the north of Auckland Hill into the Pacific beyond Schooner Bay.

Gordon decided to camp here: twelve miles were enough for one day. And as the stream required a name he called it Stop River because of the halt on its banks.

The camp was pitched under the trees nearest the lake. The birds were reserved for breakfast, and the tucutucos formed the principal dish; and again Service performed his duties satisfactorily. The need for rest soon followed that of food, and as the mouths had opened in hunger the eyes soon shut in sleep. A large fire was lighted, before which the boys, wrapped in their blankets, stretched themselves out. Wilcox and Donagan took it in turns to watch, but the fire's bright light kept wild animals at a distance;

there was no alarm, and at daybreak all were ready to resume the journey.

But the river had not only to be named—it had to be crossed; and as it was not fordable, the Halkett boat was brought into use. It was a frail craft—able to carry but one at a time, so that the water had to be crossed from the left bank to the right seven times, and this took an hour. But the provisions and ammunition were kept dry.

Fan did not mind wetting her feet, and swam across in a few moments.

The ground being no longer marshy, the boys kept along by the lake, and after breakfast at ten off some grilled peccary they bore away northwards. There was nothing to show that the end of the lake was near, and the eastern horizon was still shut in by the circular line of water and sky.

It was not till noon that Donagan looking through the glasses, exclaimed—' There's the other coast! '

Looking in that direction they saw a few tree-tops beginning to show above the water.

'We mustn't stop,' said Gordon. 'Let's get there before night.'

An arid plain, undulating with long sandhills, dotted with a few clumps of rushes and reeds, stretched away out of sight. In this northern part it appeared as though Charman Island consisted only of vast sandy tracks, contrasting with the verdant forests of the centre; and to it Gordon appropriately gave the name of Sandy Desert.

By three the opposite coast appeared quite clearly about two miles to the north-east. There seemed to be no living creature near except the sea-birds, cormorants, petrels, and grebes, which flew over on their way to the shore.

If the schooner had been wrecked in these parts the boys would have thought they were indeed on a barren island: in vain would they have sought in the desert for their comfortable dwelling at French Den. When the shelter of the schooner failed them, they would have found no shelter here.

Need they now go further, to explore a part of the island that seemed uninhabitable? Could they not leave till later the exploration of the right bank of the lake, where the forest might be found again? Certainly. Besides, it would be on the east that they would find the American continent, if Charman Island were anywhere near it. However, at Donagan's suggestion, they resolved to gain the end of the lake, which could not be far off, for the double curve of its banks became sharper and sharper. And at nightfall a halt was made at a little creek which ran in at the north angle of Family Lake.

Here there was not a tree, not even a clump of grass, of moss, or dry lichen. The boys had to content themselves with the provisions they had brought, and as there was no shelter, they had to sleep under the stars on the bed of sand. And nothing came to trouble the silence of the night.

CHAPTER XV

BRAVO, BAXTER!

TWO HUNDRED yards from the creek there was a hill about fifty feet high; this served as an observatory, from which Gordon and his comrades might have an extended view of the country. And as soon as the sun rose they climbed this hill.

The glasses were directed towards the north. If the sandy desert stretched away, as the map showed, it was impossible to ascertain its boundary line, for the sea horizon would be about twelve miles to the northward, and more than seven to the eastward. There seemed to be no good in going further north.

'Then,' asked Cross, 'what are we to do?'

'Go back,' Gordon decided.

'Not before breakfast,' Service pleaded.

'Get the cloth laid,' said Webb.

'If we're going back,' Donagan asked, 'couldn't we go another way?'

'We'll try to,' Gordon agreed.

'It seems to me,' Donagan suggested, 'that we should complete our exploration if we went along the other bank of the lake.'

'That would be rather long,' Gordon reminded him. 'According to the map that must be from thirty to forty miles, and it would take four or five days supposing we met with nothing to stop us! At French Den they'd be very anxious about us.'

'But,' Donagan reminded him, 'sooner or later we'll have to explore that part.'

'Certainly,' Gordon agreed: 'and I intend to send an expedition over there.'

'But,' said Cross, 'Donagan is quite right in not wanting to go back the same way.'

'Quite so,' Gordon agreed, 'and I mean to follow the lake shore to Stop River, and then to strike off for the cliff, and skirt it on our way to the caves.'

'And why go down the river?' asked Wilcox.

'Why indeed?' said Donagan. 'Why not make a short cut across the sand to the first trees in Trap Woods, which aren't more than three or four miles to the southwest?'

'Because we have to cross Stop River,' Gordon answered. 'We know we can get across where we crossed yesterday; but farther down we might find a torrent that would give trouble. If we enter the forest on the left bank of the river, we're bound to be all right.'

'Always cautious, Gordon!' Donagan exclaimed with just a touch of irony.

'You never can be too cautious!' said Gordon.

And then they all slipped down the hill, regained their camp, ate a little biscuit and cold venison, rolled up their blankets, and started back on the road they had come along the night before.

The sky was magnificent. A light breeze barely ruffled the surface of the lake. There was every sign of a fine day. If the weather would only keep fine for thirty-six hours Gordon would be satisfied, for he counted on reaching French Den the next evening.

By eleven the boys were back at Stop River. Nothing had occurred on the way except that Donagan had shot two splendid tufted bustards, with a plumage of black mixed with red above and white below, which put him in as good a humour as Service, who was always ready to pluck, draw, and roast any bird whatsoever.

This was the fate of the bustards an hour later, when the boys had crossed the river in the Halkett boat.

'Now we're under the trees,' said Gordon, 'and I hope Baxter will have a chance of using the lasso or the bolas.'

'He hasn't done much with them as yet,' Donagan did not think much of any weapon of the chase except firearms.

'And what could we do with the birds?' asked Baxter.

'Birds or quadrupeds, Baxter, I don't think much of your chance.'

'Nor I,' added Cross, always ready to support his cousin.

'You might as well wait until he's tried them before you condemn them,' said Gordon. 'I am sure he'll do something good. When our ammunition gives out, the lasso and the bolas won't fail us.'

'But the birds will,' said Donagan.

'We'll see,' said Gordon, 'and now let's have lunch.'

But the preparations took some time, as Service wanted his bustard cooked to a turn. The one bird was enough for the meal; it was a good-sized one, and these bustards weigh about thirty pounds, and measure nearly three feet from beak to tail, being among the largest specimens of the feathered tribe. This one was eaten to the last mouthful, and even to the last bone, for Fan, to whom the carcase fell, left as little as her masters.

Lunch being over, the boys started off into the unknown part of Trap Woods traversed by Stop River on its way to the ocean. The map showed that it curved towards the northwest to get round the cliff, and that its mouth was beyond False Point; so Gordon decided to leave the river, which would take him in the opposite direction to French Den, his object being to take the shortest road to Auckland Hill, and then strike northwards along its base.

Compass in hand, he led the way to the west. The trees, wider apart than in the more southerly district, offered no obstacle, and the ground was fairly clear of bushes and underwood.

Among the birches and beeches opened little clearings into which the sunlight shone. Wild flowers mingled their fresh colours with the green of the foliage and the carpet of grass. In places, superb senecios bore their blooms on stems two or three feet high, and Service, Wilcox, and Webb gathered some of the flowers and stuck them in their coats.

Then it was that a discovery of great use was made by Gordon, whose botanical knowledge was often to be useful to the little colony. His attention was attracted by a very bushy shrub, with poorly developed leaves and spiny branches, bearing a reddish fruit about the size of a pea.

'That is the trulca, if I'm not mistaken,' said he. 'It's a fruit much used by the Indians.'

'If it's eatable,' Service replied, 'let's eat it, for it won't cost anything.'

And before Gordon could stop him Service began to crack some of the fruit between his teeth. He made a horrible grimace, and his comrades roared with laughter, while he spit out the abundant salivation caused by the acid on his tongue.

'You told me it was eatable!' he exclaimed.

'I didn't say it was eatable,' replied Gordon. 'The Indians use the fruit for making a drink by fermentation.

The liquor will be of great value to us when our brandy has all gone, that is if we mind what we are doing with it, for it soon gets into the head. Fill a bag with the trulcas, and we'll experiment with them at French Den.'

The fruit was not easy to gather from among the thousands of thorns, but by beating the branches Baxter and Webb knocked enough on to the ground to make a bagful and then the journey was resumed.

Farther on, the pods on another shrub were also gathered. They were the pods of the algarrobe, another South American native, which also ferment and yield a strong liquor. This time Service abstained from trying them, and he did well, for although the algarrobe seems sweet at first, yet it soon makes the mouth extremely dry.

In the afternoon, a quarter of a mile before they reached Auckland Hill, the boys made another discovery of quite as much importance. The nature of the forest had changed. In the more sheltered position, the vegetation was more richly developed. Sixty or eighty feet from the ground the trees spread their huge branches, among which innumerable song-birds chattered. One of the finest of the trees was the antarctic beech, which keeps its tender green foliage all the year round. Not quite so high, but still magnificent, rose clumps of 'winters,' with bark the flavour of cinnamon.

Near there Gordon recognised the 'pernettia,' the tea-tree of the whortleberry family, met with in high latitudes; an infusion of its aromatic leaves yields a very healthy drink.

'That will take the place of our tea,' said Gordon. 'Take a few handfuls of the leaves, and later on we'll come back and gather enough for the winter.'

It was four o'clock before Auckland Hill was reached

near its northern end. Although it did not seem to be as high here as at French Den, yet it was impossible to ascend because of the extreme steepness of its slope. This was, however, of no consequence, as it was intended to follow its base all the way to Zealand River.

Two miles farther on the boys heard the murmur of a torrent which foamed through a narrow gorge in the cliff, and which was easily forded.

'This ought to be the stream,' Donagan suggested, 'the one we discovered on our first expedition.'

'The one with the causeway?' asked Gordon.

'Yes,' said Donagan, 'the one we called Dike Creek.'

'Well, let's camp on its right bank,' said Gordon. 'It is just five, and if we're to pass another night in the open air, we might as well do it here under the shelter of these big trees. Tomorrow, I hope, we'll sleep on our beds in the hall.'

Service busied himself preparing the second bustard for dinner. It was to be roasted like the other one; but it is not fair to find fault with Service on account of the sameness of his bill of fare.

While dinner was being got ready, Gordon and Baxter strolled off into the wood, one in search of new plants, the other meaning to use his lasso or his bolas—if it were only to put an end to Donagan's jokes.

They had gone about a hundred yards into the thicket, when Gordon, calling Baxter by a gesture, pointed to a group of animals playing about on the grass.

'Goats?' asked Baxter, in a whisper.

'Yes, or rather animals that look like goats,' said Gordon. 'Try and get one—'

'Alive?'

'Yes, alive; it's lucky Donagan isn't with us. He would

have shot one before now, and put the others to flight! Let's get nearer quietly and don't let them see us.'

There were six of these goats, and they had not yet taken alarm. One of them, a mother probably, suspecting some danger, was sniffing the air and looking about, ready to clear off with the herd.

Suddenly a whistling was heard, the bolas came spinning from the hand of Baxter, who was not twenty yards from the group. Well aimed and thrown, it wound round one of the goats, while the others disappeared into the thicket. Gordon and Baxter ran towards the goat, which was vainly trying to escape from the bolas. She was seized so that it was impossible for her to get away, and two kids, that instinct had kept near the mother, were also taken prisoners.

'Hurrah!' joy had rendered Baxter demonstrative. 'Hurrah! Are they goats?'

'No' answered Gordon. 'I think they are vicugnas.'

'And will they give milk?'

'Oh, yes.'

'Then hurrah for the vicugnas.'

Gordon was right. Although the vicugnas resemble goats, their paws are longer, their fleece is short and fine as silk, their head is small and has no horns. They chiefly inhabit the pampas of America, and even the country round the Magellan Straits.

We can easily imagine how Gordon and Baxter were welcomed when they returned to the camp, one leading the vicugna by the cord of the bolas, the other carrying a kid under each arm. As their mother was still nourishing them, it was probable that the youngsters could be brought up without difficulty. They might be the nucleus of a herd that would become very useful to the colony.

Donagan doubtless regretted the splendid shot he had missed; but when the game had to be taken alive, he had to admit that the bolas was better than the gun.

The boys dined, or rather supped, in high spirits. The vicugna, tied to a tree, did not refuse to feed, while the kids gambolled round her.

The night, however, was not so quiet as the one spent in Sandy Desert. This part of the forest was visited by animals more formidable than jackals, and their cries were recognisable as being a combination of howling and barking at once. About three in the morning there was an alarm due to some growling close by.

Donagan, on guard near the fire, gun in hand, did not think it worth while to wake his comrades, but the growling became so violent as to wake them itself.

'What's the matter?' asked Wilcox.

'There are some wild beasts prowling round,' Donagan explained.

'Probably jaguars or cougars!' Gordon suggested.

'One is as bad as the other.'

'Not quite, Donagan, the cougar is not so dangerous as the jaguar: but in a pack they're dangerous enough.'

'We're ready for them,' said Donagan. And he put himself on the defensive, while his comrades got out their revolvers.

'Don't shoot until you can't miss,' Gordon told them. 'I think the fire will keep them off.'

'They're close by,' said Cross.

And the pack was near enough, to judge by the fury of Fan, whom Gordon had some difficulty in holding back. But it was impossible to distinguish any form in the deep darkness of the forest.

Evidently the creatures were accustomed to come and

drink at night in this place. Finding their haunt occupied they showed their displeasure by their frightful growls.

Suddenly, moving spots of light appeared some twenty yards away. Instantly there was the report of a gun.

Donagan had fired, and a storm of growls replied. His comrades, revolver in hand, were ready to shoot if the wild beasts should rush the camp.

Baxter, seizing a burning brand, hurled it straight at the glittering eyes; and instantly the growling stopped, and the animals, one of whom should have been hit by Donagan, were lost in the depths of Trap Woods.

'They've moved off,' said Cross.

'Good luck to them,' exclaimed Service.

'Will they come back?' asked Cross.

'That isn't likely,' said Gordon; 'but we'll watch till daylight.'

Some wood was thrown on the fire, which was kept blazing till the day broke. The camp was struck, and the boys ran off into the thicket to see if one of the animals had been killed.

They found the ground stained with a large patch of blood. The brute had been able to get away, and it would have been easy to recover if Fan had been sent in search of it, but Gordon did not think it worth while to go further into the forest. The question arose as to whether they were jaguars or cougars or something just as dangerous, but after all the important point was that the boys were all safe and sound.

At six they were off again. There was no time to lose if they were to cover during the day the nine miles between them and French Den.

Service and Webb took care of the young vicugnas,

while the mother was quite satisfied to follow Baxter, who led her with the rope.

There was not much variety in the road. On the left was a curtain of trees, some in impenetrable masses, some in scattered clumps. To the right ran the rocky wall, striped here and there with pebble bands in the limestone, and rising higher and higher as the travellers went southwards.

At eleven the first halt was made for lunch; and on this occasion, so as to lose no time, the provisions in the bags were attacked. After the fresh start was made progress was more rapid, and nothing occurred to stop it, until about three in the afternoon the report of a gun echoed among the trees.

Donagan, Cross, and Webb, accompanied by Fan, were a hundred yards in advance, and their comrades could not see them, when they heard the shout of 'Look out!'

Suddenly an animal of large size came rushing through the thicket. Whirling his lasso over his head, Baxter took a flying shot. The noose fell over the animal's neck, but so powerful was it that Baxter would have been dragged away if Gordon, Wilcox and Service had not hung on to the end of the line, and whipped it round the trunk of a tree.

No sooner had they done so than Webb and Cross appeared from under the trees, followed by Donagan, who exclaimed in a tone of ill-temper, 'Confound the beast! How could I have missed it?'

'Baxter didn't miss it,' Service told him, 'and here we have it all alive oh!'

'What does it matter?' asked Donagan. 'You'll have to kill it.'

'Kill it!' protested Gordon. 'Not at all! It's our beast of burden!'

'What, this thing?' exclaimed Service.

'It's a guanaco,' said Gordon, 'and guanacos figure largely in the studs of South America.'

Useful or not useful, Donagan was very sorry he had not shot it. But he said nothing, and went up to examine this beautiful specimen of the Charmanian fauna.

Although the guanaco is zoologically classed with the camels, at first glance it in no way resembles those animals. Its slender neck, elegant head, long, rather lanky limbs—denoting great activity—and yellow coat spotted with white, made it in no way inferior to the best horses of American descent. It could certainly be used for riding if they could tame it and break it in, as was easily done in the Argentine haciendas. It was very timid and made no attempt to escape, and as Baxter had loosened the slip-knot it was easy to lead it with the lasso, which served the purpose of a halter.

The expedition to the north of Family Lake had been profitable for the colony. The guanaco, the vicugna and her two kids, the discovery of the tea-tree, of the trulcas and the algarrobe, ensured a hearty welcome to Gordon, and even more to Baxter, who had none of Donagan's vanity and was not at all conceited over his success.

Gordon was delighted to find that the bolas and lasso could really be useful. Donagan was a capital shot, but his skill required an expenditure of powder and lead which the colony could ill spare, and Gordon determined to encourage his comrades in practising with these weapons.

The map showed that four miles still separated the boys from French Den, and the word was given to hurry on. It was not reluctance to do so which forbade Service from bestriding the guanaco and riding home in state; Gordon thought it was better to wait until the creature was broken in.

'I don't think he'll kick much,' said he, 'but if he won't let you ride, he might consent to draw the cart. Patience, Service, and don't forget the lesson we were taught by the ostrich.'

About six they arrived in sight of French Den.

Young Costar, amusing himself on the terrace, announced the approach of the expedition; and Briant and the others ran out to welcome Gordon with enthusiastic cheers.